START YOUR OWN
HOME INSPECTION
BUSINESS

PRENTICE HALL PRESS

ISBN 0-7352-0084-X

PRENTICE HALL PRESS
Paramus, NJ 07652

On the World Wide Web at http://www.phdirect.com

CONTENTS

PREFACE

Start Your Own Home Inspection Business is the result of many hours of in-depth research into one of the fastest growing opportunities in home-based business today. Our exclusive team of National Business Library's professional business writers has brought years of practical experience to this project, and we know that the information provided in this book will set you on the road to success.

Owning your own business can be the most exciting and rewarding venture you will ever experience. We talk of hundreds of small business owners who make comments like, "Doing something I really enjoy makes every day a pleasure," or "If I had known I would be realizing this kind of income, rather than making my former boss wealthy, I would have started my own business years ago."

It's true! You'll never get rich working for someone else. By capitalizing on your experience, investing time and energy, and studying the proven techniques and business methods provided in this book, you will be well on the way to realizing your goals for success in your own venture. It takes courage to begin. Without a doubt, the first step is the hardest–and you have already taken it.

INTRODUCTION:
THE DOMICILE DETECTIVE

In the time it takes you to read this book on home inspection, tens of thousands of homes will have been bought and sold. And with consumer caution at an all time high and lenders and realtors willing to do anything to make sure a sale goes smoothly, most of those homes will have been professionally inspected.

Home inspection is one of the fastest growing opportunities for home-based businesses in the United States today—with good reason. A home is the biggest single purchase that a family makes in life. And unless that family just won the Publisher's Clearing House zillion dollar giveaway, it's extremely important that they know exactly what that house will cost them now and in the future. Repairs and/or replacement of major components, such as furnaces, plumbing, electrical wiring, roofs, and other things, especially in the early years, can be devastating to a young family. Spending a couple hundred dollars on a home inspection before they buy may well save them thousands of dollars in the long term.

Who are the people who perform these professional inspections? Are they all contractors, real estate agents, or professional builders? Absolutely not. As a matter of fact, that can be a real conflict of interest. Asking a contractor to inspect your house is kind of like asking a mechanic to look over your car. In both instances it is to their advantage to find things that "need to be fixed right away!"

With realtors, it could be the opposite. They might be tempted to "overlook" anything that might jeopardize the sale. The good news is that with lawsuits as popular as they are, most realtors would not even consider doing their own inspections. They want the buyer to know exactly what they are getting. Plus, when an inspector finds a major problem, it gives the realtor bargaining power with the sellers. That's why almost any realtor, broker or mortgage banker will spring for an inspection if they can't get the owner to do it.

One of the things that makes this such a great career opportunity is the fact that as an inspector you do not have to fix anything. All you have to do is: write up mistakes in construction that are hidden to the casual observer; note code violations from original construction or add-ons; and point out potential problems that may be costly in the near future. You do not even have to suggest any particular person to fix the problems. All you have to do is find them and report them. It's that easy.

Do you think you might be the perfect candidate to be a home inspector? You're probably right. Ask yourself these simple questions. If you find yourself answering yes to most of them, then this could very well be the perfect career choice for you.

- Are you a curious person?

- Are you handy with simple tools?

- Do you enjoy disassembling things to see what makes them tick?

- Can you put the things back together!?

- Do you find yourself at the local hardware store a lot—just looking around?

- Do things like poor workmanship, and sloppy shortcuts annoy you?

- Do you like working with people?

Home inspection is not hard to learn. Naturally it requires some know how, but more importantly it requires common sense. For instance, some states require that water heaters must be secured by a flexible band in case of earthquake, high winds, etc. Other states may not require this, but it is just common sense to point out to your client that this should be done. Likewise with simple things like smoke detectors. Many people get tired of replacing batteries, so they just unhook the things. It becomes almost second nature for an inspector to write "replace batteries in all smoke detectors" on the final report. Or, if smoke detectors are missing at key spots, the inspector suggests that they be installed and points out exactly where they should be installed. It's a small cost to the client, but well worth it.

If you are already a homeowner, then you have no doubt dealt with a number of problems in your own home. Therefore, you already know some of the things to look for in other homes. The rest are easy to learn. A complete inspection takes only three to four hours, depending on the size and the age of the home. Plus, of course, a few moments to fill out the invoice! So grab your flashlight, strap on that tool belt that you've been dying to use, and let's explore this great business opportunity!

1

THE GROWTH OF
SMALL BUSINESS

The 1980s were referred to as America's "entrepreneurial era." In 1986, more than 750,000 new businesses were
created in the United States. In 1989, more than a million new ventures were started nationwide - almost half of
them by women. In 1991, there were 20.5 million small
businesses in the United States - and the entrepreneurial
era is continuing through the 1990s. The recession of the
early 1990s compelled suddenly unemployed people to
start their own businesses in order to survive. An upsurge
in part-time businesses has also fueled an entrepreneurial
trend, with people in search of extra income working on
profitable ventures during their off hours.

More and more people are opting to leave their 9-to-5
jobs and stop "making someone else" rich to focus their
energies on building a successful business of their own.
The combined circumstances of fewer advancement opportunities, lack of job security, and the possibility of retiring

without a pension are also driving the trend toward self-employment.

Today, the number of individuals who are self-employed is at its highest level ever, and based on your interest in this book, it's quite possible that you'll be joining the ranks of small business owners in the near future. It may be simply a dream right now, but that's how these businesses start.

Starting and operating your own small business is one of the most exciting and satisfying challenges you can undertake. There are no limitations on income potential when you're investing time and energy in your own enterprise. With the practical information provided in this book and dedication to your business goals, your chances for success are excellent.

What Is a Small Business?

The majority of businesses in the United States today are classified as small business. The definitions of what constitutes a small business run the gamut from the size of the overall staff (typically under 100) to the amount of assets or sales volume. However, in this book, small business is defined as one that is independently owned and operated.

The major benefit of this type of business is that you have the ability to make decisions quickly and act on them immediately. What typically bogs down big business is the number of people involved in the decision-making process.

Other advantages include the fact that small businesses can provide personalized service to the community or the market they're serving and the owner has the freedom, independence, and control to operate exactly as he or she chooses.

It's important to remember, however, that most major corporations, from Ford Motor Company and McDonald's to Mary Kay Cosmetics, started out as small businesses - as dreams.

It was because of basic business sense and a willingness to learn and adapt as their companies grew that Henry Ford, Ray Kroc, and Mary Kay, and thousands like them, steered their dreams into monumental financial successes.

Whether your goal is to supplement an existing income and to operate a solely owned home-based business from your garage, kitchen table, or spare bedroom, or to start a business that involves raising substantial capital, finding and setting up a commercial location, and hiring employees, you have the potential to enjoy an independent lifestyle that carries with it a number of rewards. And the rewards are as varied as the people who pursue them.

Accepting the Challenge

Remember, these rewards do not come without hard work and the willingness to research and understand all facets of running your business. Many new businesses fail within the first few years.

Reasons given for the early demise of a small business range from lack of organization or management experience to undercapitalization, misunderstanding of the importance of advertising, inexperience in pricing products and services, lack of an overall business plan, improper hiring practices, and failure to accurately assess the competition.

It isn't that someone purposely starts a business without having explored these areas. However, many times a person feels that his or her demonstrated expertise while in the employ of another can easily be transferred into a personal business. This is only partially true.

While it is imperative that you have particular skills or talents - because selling them is what your ultimate success will be based on - it's equally important to understand how to sell them, to know exactly what your profit margin is, and what steps you need to take to ensure the continued growth of your business.

Sounds easy, right? It really can be. But like anything else worth doing, starting your own business means careful planning. For example, you wouldn't consider taking a month-long vacation without doing some serious planning to ensure that the house was taken care of while your were gone, that you had made reservations for lodging, tours,and flights, and that you had converted your cash into traveler's checks.

There are so many aspects involved in running a business, it is vital to be prepared for any eventuality. Being prepared means being informed, so that when situations do arise you know how to deal with them.

Is "Failure" Really Failure?

We have all heard stories about people who started their businesses on a shoestring and who became successful because of their sheer determination to make it work. It does happen, but these people are the exception rather than the rule, and in most cases have had experts standing behind them to give them guidance when problems came up. Others fail and, unfortunately, this often holds potential new business owners back. We hear and read about amazingly high figures related to so-called business failures.

According to a research project conducted by Albert Shapero, professor of the American Free Enterprise System at Ohio State University for many years, no one really knows the true failure rate of new businesses. The main reason for this is because there is not really a standard definition of "failure" in this case. He points out that a number of businesses close for a variety of reasons, many of which are not documented.

For example, in some cases the owners reach retirement age and have no one to pass the business along to; others shut down because the owners simply get bored; while still other entrepreneurs file a Chapter 11 bankruptcy, which basically gives them the opportunity to stay in business and continue operating under a court-approved plan, even though they become a statistic on the "failure" list.

The other extremely important aspect to consider when thinking about the benefits and risks of starting your own business is that having a business fail has never been a deterrent for true entrepreneurs. Many well-known business moguls failed at least once, and often more than once, before striking it rich.

Learning from Experience

In fact, almost anyone who has had a business fail will tell you that the experience was more valuable than anything they could have been taught in a business school, and that it provided them with the knowledge they needed to start another venture successfully. This kind of determination is a valid qualification for self-employment and will pay off handsomely.

When you own your own business, you are responsible for everything. There will be times, such as when your accounts receivable are running sixty days late or the phone company puts the wrong number in your Yellow Pages listing, when returning to the 9-to-5 world will seem like a tempting option.

This is where self-discipline, an unwavering belief in your product or service, and the determination to be your own boss will pull you through.

But, again, we can't stress enough the importance of planning, understanding basic business practices, being aware of consumer trends, and taking the time to develop, implement, and update goals to ensure success for your efforts.

What This Book Offers

This book is designed to provide you with the information you will need to start your Home Inspection business, to offer techniques to help you with day-to-day operations, and to provide anecdotes about people just like you who had a dream and, through planning and determination, were able to turn that dream into a successful reality.

In addition to focusing on aspects of the Home Inspection business, we cover such important business matters as:

- Recognizing the entrepreneurial profile
- Taking our exclusive Entrepreneurial Quiz
- Finding the right audience for your business through easy marketing techniques
- Organizing for efficiency
- Recognizing legalities
- Addressing financial concerns
- Getting your home office up and running
- Charting your enterprise's growth

You will find specific how-to information on

- Advertising and promoting your business
- Finding capital
- Saving money on operating expenses
- Developing a simple bookkeeping system that will show you whether you're facing a financial crisis or realizing a profit

You're never too young, too old, too busy, or too poor to start a business. Owning your own business means taking advantage of our marvelous system of free enterprise. Earning a substantial living and, even better, realizing a profit for doing something that you enjoy is the American dream come true.

The opportunities for entrepreneurs have never been better. Armed with a solid product or service to sell, the determination to succeed and, most important, business know-how, there is nothing that can stand in your way.

Notes

Key Points:

_____

_____

_____

_____

Personal Thoughts:

_____

_____

_____

_____

_____

_____

_____

_____

Additional Research:

_____

_____

_____

_____

2

THE RIGHT STUFF:
THE ENTREPRENEURIAL PROFILE

Starting a business is one thing: making it work is another. We know that success in self-employment is largely the result of careful planning and understanding basic business techniques and formulas.

It is equally important that you start a business based on your expertise in a specific field and focused on your involvement in an area that you thoroughly enjoy. As many successful entrepreneurs claim, making money doing something you love is the best way to ensure a profitable future. It is always easier to address the inevitable business challenges that crop up when you are, at bottom line, creating a product or providing a service that gives you a sense of pleasure and personal satisfaction.

Personality is also a factor in determining what kind of business to get involved in, the way you will eventually set up the legal structure (sole proprietorship, partnership, etc.) and how you will run the business on a day-to-day basis. For example, if you are planning to start a business that is based on your artistic or creative abilities, it is possible that your personality is not suited to the very important aspect of sales. But without strong selling abilities there is a likelihood that your goal of distributing, for example, your hand-carved wooden boxes nationally will not come to fruition.

This isn't to say that you should decide against going into business for yourself. It simply indicates it would be in your best interest to join forces with someone who does have strong selling skills, who believes in the product as much as you do and will work toward a common goal.

On the other hand, if your personality is geared to working with people, it is a good idea to consider a business that will emphasize this ability, such as developing seminars or workshops based on your area of expertise, providing independent counseling or tutoring, or a service such as gift basket designing, which depends on your interaction with people on a one-to-one or on a group basis for success.

Self-motivation, otherwise known as drive, is one of the most important personality traits of successful entrepreneurs. This is the characteristic that gets you going and keeps you moving when you are in business for yourself. It's what helps you to keep turning out those craft items, upgrading your technical skills or developing new and improved promotional techniques when business is slow. It's what gives you the tenacity and confidence to call on a potential client even though they have told you "No" three times.

Self-motivation is also what helps you overcome the fears and concerns that inevitably arise when you own your own business. It is the main ingredient that has spurred on those people we hear about who have achieved success despite drawbacks, such as minimal capital, lack of education or limited experience.

People with a high degree of self-motivation see the greatest obstacles, such as learning a new aspect of business management, as a new and exciting challenge to overcome. If you've ever undertaken a project without fully understanding the mechanics involved in performing the task or knowing what the outcome would be, you were operating on self-motivation—the conviction that you would be able to learn whatever needed to be done to accomplish your goal.

And regardless of the outcome of the project, you undoubtedly gained more experience and knowledge than you had before, which only works to increase your sense of motivation to handle new challenges.

Research shows that the true entrepreneur should possess the following kinds of personality traits in order to be able to address the many and varied situations that arise in business ownership:

Ten Traits of Successful Entrepreneurs

1. **Motivation**
(Self-driven, goal-oriented)

2. **Confidence**
(Belief in oneself & one's goals)

3. **Self-Awareness**
(Cognizance of one's positives & negatives)

4. **Courage**
(Separates the entrepreneur from the dreamer)

5. **Curiosity**
(The constant need to increase awareness)

6. **Optimism**
(Expectant, forward-looking)

7. **Flexibility**
(Adaptable to changing needs)

8. **Decisiveness**
(Able to make quick, wise decisions)

9. **Patience**
(With people as well as circumstances)

10. **Drive**
(The unquenchable desire to succeed)

The willingness to take risks. Courage is a valuable trait when striving for success. We have heard successful people say something similar to this: "I don't know how I did it; I just made a phone call and asked for the money I needed." It was more than luck that made it possible for this person to raise the capital they needed to get their business off the ground; it was the willingness to take a chance—in this case, the risk that they would receive a positive response to the request.

The owner of a small cabinet-refinishing business said, "I always figure that the worst thing that can happen is someone will say no, so it never hurts to try." In the game of business, you must be willing to take chances. Even if you don't get exactly what you want every time, the odds are good that if you feel strongly about what you need, you will get it. But you have to ask!

Confidence. The age-old philosophy of positive thinking is a step in the direction of success. By behaving as if you already are a success at what you do, it follows that you will be, and your customers will believe it too. A confident attitude is one of the most appealing traits you can exhibit to a prospective client, for it lets them know that they will be getting the best their money can buy.

Patience. When you own your own business, there will be moments when you feel like the roof is caving in, especially when your suppliers seem to be taking their own sweet time in fulfilling an important order or when a customer's demands seem to be unrealistic. Although you may be able to hurry the supplier along, you must remember that your customers are always right, since they are the ones who can financially make or break your business.

If you are aware that patience is not a strong suit, develop a stop-gap exercise for yourself to use at times when coping is a definite necessity. Whether its the time-honored "count to ten before saying a word" theory, visualizing a pleasant scene or repeating a secret phrase to yourself when tension is running high, it will be to your advantage.

Decision-making. Business has been described as a process of making one fast decision after another. Often, a decision has to be made immediately, on the spur of the moment. In those instances, you should go with your intuition and trust that you are doing the right thing.

However, if you are the type of person who prefers to analyze your options, weigh all the factors and make decisions slowly, then that is what you must do. It will not only keep your confidence intact, but will ensure that you're taking the right action. Again, careful planning will help you predict many of the decision-making situations arising in business. As time goes by and you grow more comfortable in your role as business owner, you'll find yourself making faster decisions.

> *You have to accept whatever comes, and the important thing is that you meet it with courage and with the best you have to give.*
>
> *Eleanor Roosevelt*

Experience. The results of a Dun & Bradstreet survey conducted a few years back indicated that a primary reason some businesses fail within a few years of start-up is "incompetence in the area of business experience." Whether or not your experience is directly related to the business you're planning to start, it's a key component for growth.

If you feel you don't have enough business experience, there are several avenues you can take before starting your own enterprise. Returning to school for specialized courses is one answer. Most community colleges and adult education facilities offer classes and seminars in business start-up and maintenance these days. There are also hundreds of courses available to you by mail—over 1,200 schools and universities now offer home study or correspondence courses that will, in many cases, give you official certification in your field.

However, your best solution is to take a job in the field

you're interested in. By asking questions about all aspects of the business, you will gain experience, get paid for learning and find out whether this is really what you want to do—before sinking money, time and energy into the enterprise.

Perseverance. One of the adages you will hear time and time again when talking to entrepreneurs is that perseverance is 90 percent of the battle to succeed. If you are like the majority of new small business owners, the entire staff and support system for your venture is probably you. Making a dream come true can be a lonely task, especially when you are just getting started, and ensuring that it works often means little rest or relaxation. You must be willing to persevere during the rough times, to hang in there during the slow periods and to maintain your belief in your product and service even when it seems like no one else in the world knows you exist. It has been written that through perseverance the snail reached the ark. So it is with success!

The Entrepreneurial A to Z Appraisal

Owning a business calls for the ability to handle different situations with confidence. The following self-appraisal quiz has no right or wrong answers. It is designed to help you in determining personality traits, attitudes and qualifications that will benefit you in your venture.

The Entrepreneurial Quiz

Use the letter *S* for strong or *N* for needs improvement beside the characteristics listed below. Give yourself sufficient time to analyze each trait. Upon completion, use the appraisal as a starting point for discussions with friends and family members about your business profile. Acknowledging the strong and weak points will help you prepare for your role as an entrepreneur.

Achievement: I have a strong desire to be successful in my chosen business venture. _____

Belief: I have a faith in myself and the service or product I am specializing in to build my business. _____

Creativity: I am able to address situations in imaginative and innovative ways to reach my goals. _____

Discipline: I am self-motivated and able to handle necessary tasks, whether or not I enjoy them. _____

Efficient: I am organized and able to arrange my priorities or change my work methods as needed for maximum production. _____

Friendly: I am genuinely interested in people and enjoy my interactions with them on a day-to-day basis. _____

Goal-Oriented: I have a tendency to set my sights on preset goals and to work hard toward them. _____

Health-Conscious: I am aware of my physical abilities and have the insight to work smart in order to preserve my health. _____

Independent: I am able to work alone, if necessary, and prefer to be responsible for my own actions. _____

Judgment: My conclusions about people or situations are generally accurate. _____

Knowledge: I have solid experience in my field and have spent enough time in a professional business setting to learn the ropes. _____

Leadership: I am able to direct people effectively while instilling confidence and loyalty. _____

Maturity: I am willing to work toward long-term goals and do not get upset by the inevitable minor setbacks. _____

Networking: I am willing to develop associations with other entrepreneurs for bilateral support in my venture. _____

Optimism: I am able to see what is right about a situation and to explore its potential to the fullest. _____

Positive Attitude: I am convinced that I can accomplish anything I decide to do and rarely entertain negative thoughts. _____

Questioning: I am not afraid to ask questions to get the information I need to expand my knowledge. _____

Resourceful: I am able to find ways to accomplish just about any task I must do. _____

Sales Ability: I can present information about myself and/or my business in a convincing yet honest manner. _____

Tolerance: I am able to handle stressful situations with a positive and realistic attitude. _____

Undaunted Spirit: I am unafraid of the unknown. In fact, I enjoy a challenge and accept the consequences of my actions. _____

Venturesome: I am not afraid of hard work to reach my goals and enjoy finding new, positive ways to handle troublesome situations. _____

Well-balanced: I generally maintain a sense of humor when things don't work out as expected. _____

Expressive: I am able to express ideas and feelings, both orally and in written form, with clarity and logic. _____

Youthful Nature: I am capable of tackling work with enthusiasm and a high level of energy. _____

Zest: I look forward to enjoying my business, the people I will be dealing with and the resulting fruits of my labor. _____

Scoring

Although this is not a test, merely a tool to provide you with information about your entrepreneurial profile, there are immediate clues to your future as a business owner in the responses you have given.

If you have indicated 15 or more "S" codes, there is a good possibility that you have been involved in your own business in the past or, at least, have worked in a managerial capacity for someone else. You have the positive personality traits required to be a successful business owner. If you have between 8 and 15 "S" responses, you are basically a positive and directed person and should not have any problem with improving certain areas to increase your personal business success potential.

If you have fewer than 8 "S" responses, this is an indication that finding a complimentary business partner who can support your goals may be an option worth considering.

3

HOME INSPECTION: HOME (AND INCOME) IMPROVEMENT

A Day in the Life of a Home Inspector

Ron Martin pulls slowly up the gravel driveway toward the two-story home. Whether he realizes it or not, he has already started his inspection with a quick once-over of the exterior of the house. The paint looks new, which is a good start, but Ron makes a mental note about the roof. From a distance it appears to be missing some wooden shakes. Probably not enough to cause leaking, but he'll know for sure when he gets in the attic.

The Stinsons—Bob and Mary—are waiting on the porch. They do not own this house yet, but they know that if they want it, they have to act right away. That's why they've called Ron. They are not even sure what a home inspection consists of, but they are ready to make a bid and they want to know if there are any problems with the house.

They shake hands all around and Ron tells them that his job is similar to that of a detective. He is going to snoop around and uncover details about how the house was built and how it is holding together. Fortunately, this house is less than 20 years old. The electrical should be up to code and it doesn't appear as if any additions have been added. That means a lot less work for Ron and less potential expense for the Stinsons.

Overview of Home Inspection

This is a labor intensive business with strong income potential and steady growth. It does not lend itself to absentee ownership and can be started from home with the owner as sole employee.

Minimum Start-up Investment:	$500
Average Start-up Investment:	$2,500
High Start-up Investment:	$7,500-$10,000
Breakeven Point:	Three to six months
Average Annual Gross Revenues:	$25,000-$40,000
Potential Annual Gross Revenues:	$75,000+

Ron decides to start at the top and work his way down, partially because he wants to check the attic for leaks while it is fresh in his mind. While he's up there he will also need to check the distance between ceiling joists, the depth of insulation, look for any faulty wiring, and look for any evidence of termite infestation. He will note all of his findings on a simple checklist. He also has a sketch pad with him. When he finds a problem, he will make a quick layout drawing so that he can point out exactly where it is.

Because this is a California home, it has no basement. It is built on a cement slab. This means that the gas furnace is in the attic. Ron takes out his flashlight and begins a visual inspection of the furnace. It appears to be in good shape, but when he checks inside using a telescoping mirror he detects some rust. He marks down on his pad that the furnace should be serviced. He also checks the filter and notes that it needs replacing. Finally he follows the heating ducts, does a visual and then asks the Stinsons to turn the heat on briefly. He does a smell test for signs of a gas leak, If he smells any gas at all, Ron will take out his gas and carbon monoxide tester and locate the leak. Improperly vented heating systems, or worn out heat exchangers can cause high levels of carbon monoxide, which can cause a shortage of oxygen and can lead to carbon monoxide poisoning. If Ron detects even the slightest levels he will mark down that the furnace must be professionally serviced or replaced immediately.

After the attic, Ron walks around the second story. He does a visual on the floors, carpet, ceiling, and walls. He looks for any sign of cracking or water marks that might indicate present or past leaking. Then, with another simple test device, Ron checks the electrical outlets. He pulls off the face plates and makes sure the outlets are properly attached to the wall studs and that the wires are in good shape. Finally, he checks the windows for ease of operation, latching and unlatching, and tightness against the elements.

In the upstairs bathrooms, he checks the ceiling fan and notes that it is dirty and has a loose wire. This is another must-fix item. He finds some minor cracking in the fiberglass shower wall and takes notes; then he turns the water on full to check the speed of the drain. He checks the toilet for leaks and flushes several time while observing the fill rate inside the tank, and how fast and completely it shuts off when full. Because, Ron recognizes that the house is equipped with a certain brand of low-flush toilets, and he knows that the rubber gaskets wear out fast on this model, he suggests that they are replaced on all units every six months to a year or whenever the water seems to run longer than normal.

Finally, Ron checks the bathroom electrical outlets to see if they have ground fault circuit interrupters (GFCIs). GFCIs are designed to shut off power immediately should something happen like an electrical device falling into a sink full of water. They also prevent shocks should someone standing in water touch the outlet. Homes that comply with the National Electrical Code are required to have GFCI protection in bathrooms (since 1975), garage wall outlets (since 1978) and outdoor receptacles (since 1973). These outlets have a test button and reset button between the two outlets, acting like an instant circuit breaker. The Stinsons' house being fairly new does contain GFCIs. In older homes, Ron suggests that the clients contact an electrician to have them installed, or at least purchase portable units which an owner can plug in themselves. This is especially crucial for outdoor outlets for those owners that employ gardeners. If an electrical device jams, it is best if the power shuts off before an employee gets injured, which could lead to a lawsuit.

Downstairs, Ron again checks the floors, walls, ceilings and carpets in each room. On his checklist he marks either Excellent, Good or Poor beside each item for each room. If he finds a particular problem, like cracks in the wall, he will write that down under Comments. Again, he will use a diagram if necessary.

In the kitchen, Ron checks all the appliances, right down to the clock on the stove. He checks under the sink for leaks and does a visual on the garbage disposal. The Stinsons' disposal has a sticker on it from a well-known national plumbing outfit, indicating that work has been done either to the plumbing or the disposal itself. Ron notes this.

He looks in all the cabinets for signs of roaches, mice and termites, as well as dampness. Then he examines the countertops for wear and cracking. Finally, he checks the hood over the stove and finds that it sounds terrible. It needs replacing—a costly item. He writes this down.

The Stinson's water heater is located in the garage. Ron checks it for evidence of leaks, to make sure it is functioning properly, and to assure that it is properly attached to the wall. The good news is that the water heater looks fairly new. Unfortunately, whoever installed it secured it with a solid band. Because in California a water heater may rock and roll occasionally during an earthquake, Ron makes note that it should have an expandable spring as part of the band. It will be less apt to break during a quake. Ron also suggests that all the gas units should have flexible copper connectors rather than solid ones that might break. Even though the unit is new, Ron checks for rust and to make sure the unit is properly vented through the garage roof.

Ron's final duties will be to check the fireplace to make sure that the damper is working properly, that the flue is clean and without cracks, that the firebricks are in good shape, and that the gas starter is working properly and not leaking. When he climbs onto the roof, he will check the chimney, the chimney cap and the chimney flashing. He will also look for any signs of blockage, including nesting animals. As is almost always the case, the chimney is dirty and Ron suggests having a chimney sweep attend to it immediately.

Ron checks the roof, notes the missing shakes, looks for any holes, although he does not expect to find any, because of the lack of any leaking. Ron checks all the gutters to make sure they are firmly attached, clear of debris, and that the original contractor installed the metal edge flashing properly to prevent water from backing up under the shakes and roof paper during heavy rains. The gutters appear to be original, showing signs of wear and rusting, and Ron notes that they may need replacing soon.

While it is not as crucial with a slab home to check the landscaping for proper drainage, Ron checks anyway. A damp floor may be the result of an improper gravel fill, which aids drainage away from the slab. Homes with basements, especially older homes, often leak because the footing drain tile is clogged, broken, or was never installed in the first place. Or, it make leak because the house has settled on loose ground causing a negative pitch.

Well, there you have it. You have just completed your first home inspection. If it were you now instead of Ron Martin, you would discuss your finding with the Stinsons and tell them you will present them with a complete report within the next day or two along with your invoice. Then you would go home, check your answering machine and maybe grab some lunch before your next adventure!

4

MARKETING YOUR
HOME INSPECTION BUSINESS

Home inspection has a specific market. In other words, advertising to the general public would be a waste of time and money. Most of your customers will be home buyers. We are definitely in the buyer beware stage of life when we purchase a home; it must be everything we want and need for a long period of time. Any buyer today that does not invest in a professional, independent home inspection is taking a huge risk.

Note that I used the term independent home inspection. This is a fantastic selling point that you can use to sell your services. When you tell potential clients that you are not a contractor and are not associated with a contractor or building firm and that your only fee will be the cost to do the inspection, they will trust you completely. You have nothing to gain by finding problems or overlooking problems. You are contracting out only to honestly inspect the house, write a detailed report and get paid.

If you are a professional builder or contractor and want to do home inspections as part of your business, that is fine also. There are buyers who want contractors to do the inspection. Then they can receive a quote on all major repairs as part of the inspection, which they can use as a bargaining chip with the seller, or as a determination factor as to whether the house is worth investing in.

Directory Access

Either way, you need to reach the home buyer. One of the best ways to do this is through the Yellow Pages of your local phone book. Typically, home inspectors advertise under "Home Inspection," Building Inspection Services," or as part of their listing under "Contractors." Ad rates vary. When you open a business phone account (which we'll discuss under Start-Up Basics) you are given a free one-line listing under the category of your choice. This type of listing can easily get lost on the page, especially if there are a number of others advertising in this same section. There are many other Yellow Page options that the local phone book publisher can offer you. For instance, you can boldface your type in all caps for $10-$15 a month. You can buy a one-inch type-only display ad for about $50 per month; add graphics for another $10 or so and color for another $25. From there you can buy larger display ads for more money per month. To decide what might be best for you, randomly open the Yellow Pages and see what grabs your attention under different headings—then look under headings you are thinking of for your own business to see what the competition is doing. When you call the phone company, tell them you like a certain ad on a certain page and they can tell you exactly how much that ad will cost per month.

The Classified Connection

Advertising in the classifieds in your local newspapers (and other neighboring newspapers) is also perfect for services. Some papers even have special sections at special rates that advertise local business services, and they offer deals for regular advertisers. Rates vary on the size and location of the newspaper. Some cities also have weeklies, which offer good rates for advertisers. Many papers have special real estate sections. This is where you want your ad. People looking for a home read these sections religiously. If there is a day of the week when the newspapers puts out a special real estate supplement (often on Sunday), advertise there. Try to negotiate a position on the right hand side of the page, fairly high up. It will be the first place someone looks when turning the page.

If you are willing to travel, look at advertising regionally in controlled circulation magazines. One trick of the trade that works pretty well is to call the publication, get all the rates and show a real interest in advertising. Then when they call to confirm just before closing deadline, explain that you just can't afford their rates. Nine times out of ten they will make you a deal just so they can fill the page. If they don't offer a deal, ask them specifically if they can give a first time advertiser a break. Usually, the classifieds sales person is at the bottom of the ladder in the sales department, and may be willing to forgo their commission to impress the ad sales manager. Most of these smaller publications will also typeset your ad for you at no charge. Make sure that you get to see a copy of the ad before publication, so that you be can be sure they spelled your name right and that the phone number is correct.

Media Kits & Personal Contact

The advertising departments of local magazines and newspapers undoubtedly have a "Media Kit" available for potential advertisers, which they will gladly send you upon request. These packets contain a breakdown of their advertising rates and specifications, a description of why advertising with them is to your benefit and, most important, a profile of their readership. A friendly conversation with one of their salespeople should give you a wealth of data.

They can give you a good run-down on trends, as well as an overview of current sales figures for their products. Since they are hoping you will eventually use them as a supplier for your business, they will be more than happy to give you free information.

It is, of course, often possible to gauge what the competition is doing and to glean information from them. There are two approaches when talking to people who are soon to be in direct competition. One is to be up-front and honest about your business plans and appeal to their sense of "industry spirit."

Surprisingly, you will find the direct approach works in the majority of cases as most people are genuinely interested in and supportive of others trying to make it in their field. It is better for everyone if "industry" standards are maintained and competitors have a healthy rapport. And, except in extreme situations such as a very small community, there is generally enough business to go around. It shouldn't be difficult to capture your share of the market, especially if you can develop something unique to attract them.

On the other hand, if competitors are less than receptive, it may be necessary to partake in a bit of super-sleuthing to get the information you want. A little brainstorming with friends should result in a few good ideas if you find it necessary to resort to investigative techniques.

Other Inspection Markets

Although buyers will be your main focus, there are many others who routinely require the services of a home inspector. Real estate agents need home inspectors to protect them from liability. It is estimated that more than three out of four claims against real estate agents involve failure to disclose construction problems. (Incidentally, this is an excellent point to use in your sales pitch to agents.) As soon as you have business cards, send one to every major real estate agent in your area.

> ### *Five Factors Used in Targeting Your Market*
>
> 1. Population
> 2. Income
> 3. Competition
> 4. Market Match
> 5. Desire

Lenders and banks often require inspections for their property transactions. If you can make a connection at a local bank or lending institution and offer them a reasonable price per inspection, based on a certain number of inspections per month, they might be the only client you need! Unless you are really good friends with your bank connection, you should approach the person with a cover letter first, then follow up with a phone call. Try to set up a one-on-one meeting. Then show up on time, well dressed and full of energy. Remember, a lot of people may be selling your same services, so you are there to sell yourself.

Other potential clients include attorneys that are handling divorces, wills and trusts, where the value of the house is very important; real estate appraisers, who cannot afford to overvalue a home; and professional relocation companies, who specialize in setting up high level executive families in homes all across the country.

Marketing Necessities

Before you can approach any of these potential clients, though, you must look like the professional you say you are. You'll want to have a complete inspection form to show them (see Operations section), so that they can see what they will be receiving as a final report. You will also want to be able to hand them a business card, a price list (on letterhead), and possibly a brochure outlining your services, with quotes from satisfied clients. The brochure can come later, but a business card/letterhead package is essential.

Business cards do not have to be fancy, but they should be professional. If you have no design skills and can't afford to hire a professional designer, then find someone else's business card you like and take it to your local print shop. Tell them you like the style and typeface, they will find something similar. Many small print shops include typesetting as part of their cost or charge a small fee for making your card. They should also have a selection of "standard" designs, which may be perfect for starting out.

Matching letterhead and envelopes are also important if you can afford them. Some stationery stores sell pre-designed packages, which include a matching brochure design, letterhead design, and envelope design that you simply run through a laser printer. This can be advantageous if you are not sure at first whether to use your own name for the business, Like Ron Martin's Home Inspection Service, or whether to use a fictitious business name, like AAA Quality Home Inspection Service.

As with all successful businesses, your most valuable advertising source will be word-of-mouth compliments about your services. This makes those first few inspections crucial. Plan on spending more time than necessary to make sure you do the job right. Explain to your client that while you may be slower, you will not be charging extra for the extra time you are putting in. They will be pleased that they are getting such thorough service at such a good price, and you will have the added confidence that you did the best job you could. Later, after you have a few inspections under your belt, you will be able to do the same quality work in less time, translating into more inspections and more money!

My Marketing List of Potential Customers

_____

_____

_____

_____

_____

_____

_____

_____

_____

_____

_____

_____

_____

_____

_____

_____

_____

_____

_____

_____

_____

_____

_____

Marketing: in General

Now that you have selected the kind of business you want to own, it is important to explore the need for it. A process called *marketing research* will provide you with the information you need to develop your business, plan methods of distribution or promotion, and set prices which are tailored to the audience you hope to attract.

In addition, your marketing research will provide you with information that will help when you are making decisions about a location, hours of operation, the specific types of services and/or products to sell and how to gear your advertising.

Identifying Your Market

The process of identifying your audience may seem to be an extremely complex process; however, you can develop a perfectly workable and valuable marketing report using the guidelines which follow and adapting them to your particular situation. Basically, there are five factors used to target the market:

Population: The number of households in the region you are considering as a target for your business is crucial as you must have a sufficient population base to produce the sales you need to generate a profit. Equally important is the circulation and age range of readers of any magazine you will be focusing your advertising on for specific products. If, for example, the readership of a particular publication were largely of retirement age, it would not fare well if you were planning to sell products for infants. It would, however, work in your favor if you were promoting health products or even gift items.

Income: Your potential customers must have the income to purchase goods and services. Consumers in the 35-65 age group generally have considerable income which they spend on household items, personal grooming and sporting goods. This is not to discount the over-65 age group, a good-size and growing segment of the nation's population which, depending on the region, will have adequate discretionary income (money after taxes and necessities) to spend, or the 18-35 age group, which would be a desirable market for clothing, personal and recreational items.

Competition: Competition shouldn't be a negative factor. Rather, it should spur you on to stretch your creativity by coming up with something brand new or a similar product or service that is superior to those being offered by the competition—either through quality, selection or price.

Product or service market match: Basically, this means that you must be able to attract those consumers whom you have the resources to serve. As an example, if your idea of the perfect business involves national distribution of your patented weight-training equipment, you must: a) reach an audience that is receptive and interested in body building through a carefully designed advertising campaign, and b) have the financing available to supply and ship the product.

Desire: Your objective is to match your product or service to the needs and desires of a particular group of consumers who will be responsive. It is often difficult to figure out exactly what your target market wants; however, through observation of what the competition is doing, it should be possible to recognize a need.

Market Research Techniques

Large corporations often have in-house marketing staffs which conduct extensive research on a continuing basis to ensure that the products or services being offered are in line with the marketplace.

Obviously, this is an expensive and time-consuming process—one that you undoubtedly want to avoid.

> *The greatest thing in the world is not so much where we stand as in what direction we are moving.*
>
> *Oliver Wendell Holmes*

Through several easy and inexpensive methods, you can find out everything you want to know about your potential market. The first step, however, is to determine exactly what information you need. It might be trends in population figures or regional economy or how many new homes were built within the last five years in your area.

The nearest Census Bureau office and your local chamber of commerce are consistently good sources for regional statistics. The reference librarian at the public library can steer you towards other local data and fact sheets which will give you the specifics you seek. Also, the Small Business Administration compiles extensive marketing information, in addition to material on operating procedures for specific types of businesses.

Check the Directory of Trade Associations at the library to find the name and address of the advisory board for your industries (or check the Resources listed at the end of this Guide). These trade boards exist to provide associates with marketing statistics, management tips and a wealth of valuable information. Often it only takes a phone call to get more details than you could ever use.

Another excellent source of information on population, income and sales figures is the annual survey of buying power published by Sales and Marketing Management Magazine, which breaks the information down by county and cities in the United States and should be available through the library.

Focus Groups

If you really want to go into depth with your marketing study, you might consider gathering together a group of people (family members, a social or church group, or friends) for a "focus" session to determine whether your product or service will match the needs of the prospective audience. This involves presenting your proposed business idea, with product samples if applicable, and creating a questionnaire that calls for specific answers from the group members.

This method is often used by major companies when they are testing new products and, in fact, there are private companies around the nation who do nothing but put focus groups together and set up testing sites in stores, shopping malls and street corners to obtain spontaneous and objective input from potential consumers.

The questions you would want to include on your questionnaire would ideally cover such aspects as how often members of the focus group have used a similar service or product in the past, what they liked about it, what they found to be unsatisfactory, how they feel it could have been improved, whether they would be willing to try another, their age, income and any specifics that relate to your proposed business.

For a home inspection business, the questions might include a breakdown of the top three reasons people in your focus group would consider using a service like yours, what type of inspection service they would purchase and what *additional* services they would like to see offered. This kind of information will give you an immediate edge on the competition when you are ready to start advertising.

Analyzing Your Research

The bottom line in conducting your research is that you want to zero in on information which provides insights on the potential for your business idea before you invest time, money and energy in setting it up.

If, for example, you were considering starting your business in a small community and your focus group information indicated that only 10 percent of the local residents would consider using it, you would definitely want to reconsider the validity of your concept or figure ways to promote it on a broader scale. On the other hand, if your marketing research pointed out that 90 percent of the population thought it was the greatest idea since sliced bread and that 50 percent would have an immediate need for it, the potential for your business would be much greater and proceeding with the idea would probably guarantee a profitable venture.

Buy an inexpensive notebook to help you keep track of your marketing data. Use a separate page for each category you are researching. The notebook will serve as your personal, ongoing market study to be reviewed and amended as your business grows and the audience you are serving changes.

Plan to update your information as new studies are published (generally an annual event) indicating changes in population, economy or buying and spending trends. Most newspapers publish synopses of local, state and federal studies of this nature, so maintaining your notebook shouldn't be a problem. You should also reserve several pages to record comments and suggestions from customers once your business is established, which will help you personalize the service to the market and keep you a step ahead of your competitors.

Spend as much time as needed to feel comfortable about your marketing project.

The important point is that the results of your research are comprehensive enough to provide you with concrete information on who your potential customers are and how you can best reach them.

Target audience:

_____

_____

_____

_____

Ideas for reaching the audience:

_____

_____

_____

_____

_____

_____

_____

_____

_____

Additional research information:

_____

_____

_____

_____

_____

_____

Review

• I have completed my entrepreneurial profile to determine my strengths and weaknesses. _____

• My friends and/or relatives have given me additional input based on the profile. _____

• I am aware of the advantages and disadvantages of going into business for myself. _____

• Time is not a problem; I can easily devote the time I'll need to build my business. _____

• The important people in my life are supportive of my decision. _____

• I have analyzed my personal cash flow to insure that I can support myself and my family for at least six months or until the business is solvent. _____

• I feel confident about my future as a business owner at this point. _____

• I know what people want as far as my business is concerned. _____

• I have conducted informal studies to determine my potential customers and understand their needs. _____

• I have analyzed the competition, know what they offer and have a general idea about their success ratio. _____

- I have done my marketing research and know how to get in touch with the audience I want to reach. _____

- I have contacted the trade association for my industry and have accumulated facts and figures regarding the pros and cons of starting my own business. _____

- I feel confident that my product or service is saleable. _____

5

LOCATION:
HOME OR COMMERCIAL OFFICE?

Home inspection could be an ideal enterprise to start from home. However, whether you'll be permitted to operate such a business from your home will depend on local zoning ordinances, perhaps your landlord, or other restrictions. Laws pertaining to the operation of home businesses vary by county and state. It's illegal to conduct a home-based business in certain counties, while in many others across the country it's acceptable as long as local requirements are met.

The Home Office

By operating all aspects of your mail order lingerie business from home, you'll save much-needed capital that would otherwise be spent on a commercial location. That money could go toward your all-important early-stage marketing.

If you live alone, you can basically set up your business anywhere that is comfortable for you. But if you share your living quarters with other people, it may be necessary to use a little creativity in planning an office area in a home-based business situation. A spare room, a basement or attic or family room can be turned into an office quite simply with the addition of a worktable or desk, shelving for storage and a telephone.

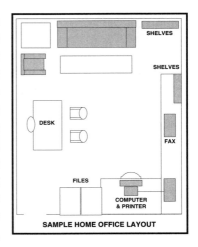

SAMPLE HOME OFFICE LAYOUT

The main consideration, once you get the business rolling, is to have a permanent base of operations so that you can leave unfinished work without disturbance and that you have a place to put supplies and business records for easy access. Do not, under any circumstances, attempt to do bookkeeping and other functions at the kitchen table or on a folding card table. You will find yourself spending countless hours having to put things away or move them somewhere else to accommodate family life.

Utilities and Phone

The home-based business has an additional advantage: Your phone line and utilities are already in place. Any additional equipment is easy to obtain from your utility carriers because you already have an established payment history.

Single-line telephone systems are adequate for most small businesses. But if your business eventually outgrows a single-line system, you'll need a multi-line system enabling you to accept several calls simultaneously and switch between lines.

Regardless of whether you need a single line or a multi-line system, some basic options are now available when choosing equipment.

Programmable memory allows automatic storage and instant dialing of phone numbers by pressing a button or entering a code.

Automatic redial reconnects the last number dialed, in some cases redialing at specific intervals until the call goes through.

Speed dialing allows you to quickly access frequently dialed numbers by using a one- to four-digit code.

Call waiting is especially useful for businesses with single lines, allowing you to take incoming calls while putting the original caller on hold.

Conference calling is often a related feature of call waiting, allowing you to simultaneously speak with two or more parties at multiple locations.

Call forwarding routes incoming calls to a pre-programmed phone number at another location.

Cordless phones are especially useful for the home business, allowing you to make or accept calls from any location in the house. Because cordless phones vary in quality, it's recommended that you thoroughly research the market before buying.

Speaker phones allow you to carry on conversations without the constraint of holding a receiver. One of the main benefits is that you can accomplish other tasks while waiting on hold. They're also useful for note-taking and similar chores during business conversations.

Voice mail is a combination answering, routing, and messaging system that can help cut front-office payroll costs while maximizing efficiency. Customers dialing a voice mail number are greeted by a recorded message and given a menu of options: direct-dialing employees in other departments; leaving messages for one or more individuals; receiving additional recorded information; and using the voice mail system with a rotary-dial phone.

The cost of voice mail has been scaled down dramatically in recent years, and is now available for small or even one-person businesses, presenting a first-class image while actually saving you money (not only in payroll costs but in avoiding potential lost revenues from unanswered or misdirected calls).

Long-Distance Carriers

Whether you're a one-person home-based operation or an expanding business in a commercial location, long-distance service is of course essential.

With AT&T, U.S. Sprint, MCI, and a host of other carriers competing for your long-distance dollar, conflicting claims and a wide range of advertised services can leave the small-business person bewildered when trying to make a choice.

> *When deciding on a long-distance carrier, consider the areas of the country and the world you'll most frequently be calling, and the monthly amount you plan to spend.*

The maze of carriers is actually two-tiered, the upper tier consisting of the major-network providers (such as AT&T) that offer direct lines to customers, and the lower tier made up of regional and national carriers that lease their lines from the major providers.

When deciding which carrier to use for your business, consider the following: the areas of the country and the world that you will most frequently be calling; the monthly amount you anticipate spending on long-distance calls;

the time of day you'll be making most of your calls; any seasonal calling patterns; and whether you'll be dealing only with clients statewide (in which case a regional WATS line would be a cost-effective choice).

In addition, read the various carriers' promotional information carefully. Does the carrier you're considering charge start-up or installation fees, or a flat monthly fee? If the latter, will you meet the carriers' minimum usage requirements, and are the services offered worth the monthly charge?

Other factors to consider include available volume discounts based on usage, and dedicated lines giving you exclusive access to a telecommunications network.

800 Numbers

Businesses that market products and services regionally or nationally have found the 800 number among their most effective marketing tools. Customers who might not otherwise pay for a call cross-country now pick up the phone without hesitation—and frequently wind up requesting further information or making hefty credit card purchases.

Though 800 numbers can pay for themselves thousands of times over, the installation fees, service charges, and usage fees can be expensive. Consider carefully whether the potential costs outweigh the benefits. An alternative is the localized 800 number, available for small, highly targeted geographic areas. Consult your phone company for further information.

Guidelines for Commercial Locations

Once volume expands to the point that operating your business from home is no longer practical, you may need to move to a commercial location.

Selecting the right location is vital to the success of your business. The first factors you must analyze when looking for a commercial location are: 1) the community you want to live and/or work in, based on family needs, finances, your preference for a particular area because of health reasons or the fact that you have an established reputation in a certain area; and 2) the locations available within that community.

These factors are interrelated. You may want to settle down in an area with a limited number of suitable business locations available. Or you may have run across a number of viable sites in several communities or areas, in which case an investigation of each must be conducted, covering each of the points listed below:

a) **The type of business you are planning to operate**. Retail, wholesale and service businesses have slightly different requirements as determined by the type of products or service being offered and the market potential in a specific area.

b) **The demographics of the area**. This includes the number of consumers who want or need your product or service and are willing and able to pay your price; the median income and employment opportunities; age ranges of the major population group; and the volume of retail trade and projected expansion data. This information is available from census reports and chamber of commerce business reports accumulated during your market research project.

c) **Competition.** You must determine how many other similar establishments are serving the market and how their businesses are going to decide if there is room for your new venture. The best way to do this is by compiling a list of businesses from the phone book that you feel will be in direct competition and, if applicable, visiting their locations at different times of day to observe the activity levels. You might also talk with employees, who should be willing to answer your questions if you approach them in a friendly way. Often, the same kind of research can be accomplished effectively on the telephone.

d) Traffic patterns. Is your proposed location close to freeways, major intersections and/or a central business district? Is there sufficient parking? Is the foot traffic past the location strong and steady enough to guarantee walk-in trade, if needed to generate sales and profits? The ease with which customers can get to your location is a major consideration in terms of success.

e) Your image. Decide on the image you want to project, such as top quality products, superior service, low prices, convenience, before you go scouting for locations.

f) The product or service. If, for example, you were planning to sell high priced, state-of-the-art European electronic equipment, it would be advisable to locate your business in a mall or on the main street of an economically comfortable community to ensure getting the response you need to survive. Generally, there are specific areas within a marketplace that cater to consumers in specific income levels and/or occupational groups, i.e., executives, blue collar workers, students, etc. Consider your product/service and the projected number of potential buyers within the community.

g) The amount of rent required. Locations having the highest potential of profit through consumer traffic (busy downtown areas, shopping malls, corner shops or stores with good frontage) are more expensive because competition keeps rents up to the maximum. The trade-off, however, is an increase in sales and, generally, a lower advertising budget because of the visibility factor.

As a new business owner, you may find that your allotted capital for rent is limited. Understanding and exploring the factors involved in selecting a location will help you find the best one for your money.

Retail Businesses

The guidelines indicated above are applicable for retail businesses. Poor location is one of the chief causes of failure among retail stores, but, on the other hand, the right location can be all it takes for even a mediocre business to thrive and grow.

Service Businesses

When clients are going to be visiting your place of business, the same principles of location selection apply as are indicated for retail. If clients will not be visiting, location selection can be based on rent, the amount of space needed and the convenience to you.

Wholesale or Manufacturing Businesses

Where you locate a wholesale business depends on your market. If dealing primarily with local retailers or customers, your location should be within easy driving distance of your clientele.

However, if most of your business is conducted through the mail or delivery services, you can base your selection on the best rent available and the convenience factor for you and your staff. When choosing a location for your wholesale business, warehousing needs are a vital consideration, as is projected expansion.

Before Signing a Lease

Unless you're planning to purchase the commercial location, rent your location from a family member or accept a temporary agreement in a location that is for sale, you will be required to sign a lease before moving in.

The most desirable agreement for you as a new business owner is a one-to-two year lease with a renewal option at a guaranteed rate for rent increases over a five to ten year period.

Rent for a commercial location is established either on a flat rate or a percentage basis. Under the flat rate, rent is generally based on the square footage of the shop and on the location or, in some cases, on potential volume. The percentage base involves a base amount of rent plus a pre-arranged percentage of monthly sales.

Your lease will also cover a number of other points, such as the liabilities and responsibilities of the landlord and of you, the tenant; i.e., who is to pay for specific repairs, renovations, tax increases and utilities, etc.

The lease may contain stipulations about the size of the exterior sign you can erect, hours of operation, insurance coverage and assignation of the lease to another party (a sublease).

Before signing a lease to set up your business, make sure that electrical lines are adequate enough to handle high volume usage, that you have restrooms for employees and/or clients, and convenient parking areas. Also check with the leasing agent to be certain you can make leasehold improvements (i.e., storage shelves, air conditioning, lighting) as the business warrants it.

It is recommended that you have an attorney review the lease carefully before you sign it to ensure that you understand all of the clauses and to serve as a negotiator, if necessary.

Inspection Location

Home Inspection is the perfect home-based business. More than 75% of your work will be performed on location at other people's homes. You can do the rest of your work, which includes preparing final reports, invoices and cover letters on the dining room table in the evenings.

You will want to eventually have your own space for your business. A space away from the disruptions of a normal household like television and kids will allow you to better concentrate on the tasks at hand.

One advantage to having your own space is that you can spread stuff out and leave it spread out as long as you need to work on it. Oftentimes, home inspectors will be given copies of the floor by floor layout of the house to study before they begin the inspection. This is a big advantage and you should ask for the plans with each new task. These plans also give you a good look at the things you can no longer see, like the footings and type of gravel fill used.

Another advantage to setting up a business office in a spare room is that you can take more tax deductions off your quarterly estimated tax returns. The law allows that you can deduct a percentage of your mortgage equal to the space that is being used exclusively for business. For instance, if you are using one room in a six room house, you may be able to deduct 1/6 of your associated housing costs. There are a number of restrictions, so be sure to either consult a tax expert or do some research at the local library.

You will almost always be meeting with clients at the house that they wish for you to inspect. Occasionally though, you may need to meet with clients in your home. This can happen with out of town clients, who may be staying with friends and do not want to impose on the friends during preliminary meetings.

It is important that you and your office look professional when entertaining clients. Again, you can bring clients into your home and sit them down at the dining room table, and you may have to do this when you start out, but almost any office space will make you appear more professional and more experienced.

One home inspector we know built a small office in his garage. He allowed enough space for his desk, filing cabinet and a large table where house plans could be spread out. He also moved a couch into the office for guests to sit on and brought in a few plants. For decoration he took high-quality photos of every home he inspected. He took the photos either in the early morning or late afternoon when the sunlight was most flattering. He used different angles and had color prints made and framed. It gave his office an inexpensive, professional look. The photos also allowed him to point out problem areas on those houses that are hidden to the untrained eye, and tell the new clients how much money he saved these previous clients. It is a great sales pitch that works almost every time.

Eventually, you may want to open an office away from home. Maybe you have noisy neighbors. Maybe there is just no space for your office. Or maybe you have become so successful that you need a place where you can hire an assistant. When this happens, choose a location for your new office that is affordable, and conveniently located. You'd be amazed how many people choose businesses of all kinds based solely on how easy it is to get to their place of business and how easy it is to park.

Many times you can find a co-operative office situation, where several professionals rent a suite of offices and share a receptionist and major equipment like copiers, fax machines and a coffee bar/lounge area. You might even consider sharing a space with complementary professionals, like architects or interior designers.

Wherever you set up your business, there are some items that you will need and others that you will want to add as you become more successful. Let's look at those items.

If setting up my business at home, I have:

- Checked with the city and county offices in my area regarding required licenses and permits and zoning regulations for home-as-office. _____
- Set aside a room or an area in my home that will be used exclusively for my business. _____
- Had a separate telephone installed and have purchased an answering machine or contracted with a message service. _____
- Set up a separate business bank account. _____
- Informed friends and family of my business routine and specific working hours to reduce interruptions and distractions. _____

If setting up in a commercial location, I have:

- Investigated rental rates for the area I am interested in. _____
- Checked traffic flow, parking and foot-traffic around my proposed location. _____
- Determined that my business is compatible with others in the area. _____
- Talked with my prospective landlord about improvements, maintenance and rent increases. _____
- Had my lawyer check the rental agreement and any local zoning regulations. _____
- Checked prices on storage units, work tables or shelves. _____
- Planned a layout that I feel will work well for the location and my storage, display and office needs. _____

6

SETTING UP YOUR BUSINESS AT HOME

There is a lot of appeal in operating your business from home.

Thousands of successful businesses have been started in a basement, a spare room or on the kitchen table. Henry Ford, for example, founded the Ford Motor Company in his garage and Jean Nidetch started Weight Watchers in her living room as a support group for friends who wanted to lose extra pounds. Both of these businesses, and many more like them, became successful multi-million-dollar corporations, despite humble beginnings.

The Small Business Administration estimates that there are close to 10 million home-based businesses in the United States today and, of these, more than 30% are owned and operated by women. These figures have been substantiated by an AT&T study, as well as by the U.S. Department of Labor.

Starting a home-based business has provided an

opportunity for many people, who might otherwise never have the chance, to become entrepreneurs. Women, especially, have discovered that they can build a profitable, satisfying business at home while still being available for their families.

For others, a home-based business is the ticket out of the world of the urban commuter. In fact, a home-based business is the perfect way to try something new to see how it works while still working another job to pay the bills. Once the business has proven itself and is realizing a profit, you can leave the job to devote full time to your new venture.

Couples often find that investing time and energy in building a business together at home develops stronger relationships in addition to increasing joint income. For the retired and for those with minor physical disabilities, it is a path to staying involved, exploring self-sufficiency and guaranteeing a profitable future.

The Advantages of Establishing a Home-Based Business

- Ability to start your business immediately
- Minimal start-up capital needed
- No rent or excessive set-up charges for utilities required
- Comfortable working conditions
- Reduced wardrobe expenses
- No commuting
- Tax benefits
- Elimination of office politics
- Flexibility and independence
- Full utilization and recognition of skills
- Low risk for trial and error

Start-Ups Never Change

As with any new business whether located at home or in a commercial location, it is important to follow the basic guidelines for start-up, including: conducting a market survey, drawing up a business plan, setting goals, reviewing capital needs and projected income, developing an advertising campaign and establishing a professional image.

Setting up your business at home automatically eliminates up to 75 percent of the start-up costs and responsibilities required for an office or storefront operation. You are, in your home, already making rent or mortgage payments and paying for your own telephone service, insurance and utilities.

In many instances, a commercial location will require $10,000 just to open the doors with basic leasehold improvements and/or equipment. In addition, valuable time and energy is saved in scouting for the location, having utilities installed and decorating the premises.

Getting Your Feet Wet

A home-based business gives you the opportunity to test the waters with a minimum of risk. This is especially beneficial to first time entrepreneurs, who may prefer to learn and grow with the business in the comfort of home without the pressures that operating out of a commercial location often brings.

As a hedge against inflation, the home-based business is a natural. In addition to low start-up, tax deductions (for use of your home as an office and your business expenses) provide relief from a seemingly endless outflow of cash on mortgage or rent payments. You must, however, be aware of the tax laws, which allow deductions only for that part of the home "used exclusively and regularly" for business and, as of last year, limited to a modified net income of the business.

After the business is running smoothly, you will find that the potential to earn money is greater because of reduced overhead. Your production will increase because you have more control over your schedule and fewer of the typical interruptions that arise in a commercial setting. Generally, home-based entrepreneurs claim that an added benefit is reduced stress, despite the fact that they are working long hours.

Of course, as with any business arrangement, there are also disadvantages to setting up your business in your home. By recognizing them, however, it is possible to address and minimize the problems before they come up.

Getting to Work

One of the biggest problems faced by home-based entrepreneurs is being able to establish a productive work schedule. There are different types of interruptions that come up in a home environment, including visits from friends and neighbors, household chores that need to be done, the temptation of television and the daily paper when there is work to be produced. There is also no one around to spur you on.

A helpful suggestion for getting down to work is to dress in the morning as if you were going out to a regular job. This alone will help you set your priorities for the day.

The best solution, however, is to establish regular working hours from the onset (although you do have the flexibility as a home-based business owner to arrange your schedule around the times you know you are the most productive). If friends want to visit, politely explain to them that you are operating a business which requires your full concentration and arrange a suitable time to get together according to your schedule.

It is also important, if you have family, that they are supportive and willing to arrange their lives as much as possible around your schedule. This can be dealt with through frequent family discussions about what you are doing and how the business operates.

Another difficult area is learning to separate business and pleasure. A home-based business often makes it very easy to work day and night on a project. Again, it is important to allot time for personal activities. The secret to remember is that the work will get done much more efficiently if you are relaxed and rested.

It's also a good idea to have the business set up in a separate room or area that can be shut off from your personal living space after working hours. This will more easily enable you to separate work from leisure time.

Home-based business owners often experience feelings of isolation from those in their industry.

One way to eliminate this is to join local groups, such as the chamber of commerce and networking groups, and to, at least, attend the meetings. Check to see how many members are entrepreneurs, which will give you a built-in support system. By making yourself available to serve on committees, you'll be able to reach into the community and publicize your business for the cost of your involvement.

The Disadvantages of Establishing a Home-Based Business

- Success is based 100% on your efforts
- Difficulty in establishing solid work habits
- Difficult to know how to set competitive rates
- Limited support system
- Isolation
- Limited work space
- Disruption of personal life
- Clients are uncomfortable coming to your home
- Zoning restrictions

Reviewing Local Laws

Before getting started, it is important to check that zoning ordinances in your area will allow you to use your home for business purposes. Since zoning ordinances vary from city to city and county to county, it is necessary to contact the Planning Department of your regional government offices or talk with your attorney to find out what is allowed. Regulations are based on the type of business, the area to be used within your home, noise control, tax regulations, business signs and other aspects. You may also need a special permit or license.

If you are expecting clients to visit your home for business, it is best to have a separate room set up as an office so that when they come to discuss a purchase, they won't feel as if they are intruding on a family. If, however, an office is out of the question, make sure you arrange meetings during times when the family is away from home to ensure that there will be no interruptions.

> *God gives every bird its food, but he does not throw it in the nest.*
>
> *J. G. Holland*

Another option is to go to the client's location when you must have meetings or to offer pick-up and delivery service, if applicable. Depending on the business, however, and the quality of your work, client discomfort shouldn't be a major problem, according to a number of home-based business owners we have interviewed.

As an example, the number of home-based typesetting services has increased dramatically over the past few years and we have never heard of any complaints or problems in this area. The bottom line, as far as the customer is concerned is still—and will always be—reliable service or high quality products and the knowledge that they are dealing with a professional.

The benefits of a home-based business to the beginning entrepreneur can mean the difference between working for someone else or turning a dream into reality.

The key element, as with any business, is motivation, a needed product or service, careful planning and the desire to succeed. But sometimes, just knowing that the expenses of establishing a business in a commercial location are alleviated by setting up a home-based enterprise is enough to push you forward to success, one small step after another.

7

START-UP BASICS:
HOME INSPECTION BASICS

We have already alluded to some of the things you will need to run your own home inspection business. Following is a comprehensive list. Some items may not be necessary right away, that's up to you to decide. It is always better to start out small and work your way up, than to overextend yourself financially. We have tried to include a range of prices and suggestions as to where to buy certain things to save money starting out. You can apply these same methods to things that might not be on the list.

Telephone

The telephone will be your most used business tool and as you become more established, your phone will be ringing when you're not there. The simplest solution of course is to have a good quality answering machine. Make sure you leave the message on the machine. While it may tickle your friends when they hear your four-year-old answer with the theme from Barney playing in the background, it could cause clients to think they have the wrong number!

The best solution is to have your own business phone line put in. Installation varies from location to location, and may be based on the age of your existing line. Budget $150 to $200 for the line, a phone and an answering machine. A business line does charge you by the minute for all calls—even local calls. But what you can do is make all your outgoing local calls on your home phone and just use your business line as a receiver.

There is another advantage to a business line—you can write off all the charges on your taxes as legitimate deductions. And, if you have a business line, the government even lets you write off any business calls that were made on your home phone. Purchasing a business line also entitles you to a free listing in the Yellow Pages under whatever heading you choose.

Fax Machine

More and more people are relying on fax machines. Many people have them in their homes, some executives even have them in their cars.

While you will always want to take a person to person meeting if you can get it, because it is much easier to sell yourself that way—many real estate agents or banking officials may be too busy to meet with you right away. If a potential client asks for a price list, you can put it their hands immediately after you talk to them. Then you can follow up with a printed copy by mail and add some associated materials like your business card and a simple brochure if you have one, perhaps include a list of some of your previous clients. Whenever you do fax or send something, make sure you follow up with a phone call several days later.

The other advantage to having a fax machine of course is receiving materials. If a client calls you and wants you to put together a quick quote, and the house is fifty miles away, you will have to jump in your car and drive there for further information. If they have an architectural sketch or photo it can be faxed to you and reviewed—saving you hours of non-billable drive time.

There are a number of good, relatively inexpensive fax machines on the market for $200-$350. Some even come with an answering machine built in so you have a combination phone, fax and answering machine. Again, if you have this hooked to your business line, you can write off all of the charges on your taxes. You can also write off the entire cost the same year you buy it. Because it is under $500, you do not have to amortize it over five years or more like more expensive items.

Computer

Speaking of more expensive items... We live in a computerized world. And it's pretty hard to run a business today without a computer. You need to send off professional-looking correspondence, invoicing, and reports at the end of your projects. A computer will make all these things much easier.

Several home inspectors we talked with have their field reports in a computer file. They take a copy with them and mark all over it, but then when they get back to the office they type the information onto a fresh copy in the computer and print out a professional-looking report. They also have a complete copy of every inspection they've done conveniently filed in a computer file.

Your computer doesn't have to be a top of the line model. It doesn't even have to be new. There are some great used computers listed in the classifieds every day, as well as for sale at computer shops and computer shows. One big advantage to buying a used computer is that oftentimes it comes already loaded with hundreds of dollars worth of software. There are a few things to watch out for, though:

• Make sure the computer is not so old that it can't be updated. By updated it should be able to take additional memory and programs added as your business grows.

• Make sure the software is common and compatible. It doesn't have to be the latest version, but it should be a recent version of one of the popular programs, like Microsoft Word or WordPerfect for word processing. Excel, Quicken, or Lotus for accounting software.

• Try to get the manuals with both the computer and software. You'll be amazed at how much you can figure out about accounting software by reading a few short paragraphs, or going through the tutorial.

• Buy a good printer. There are a lot of people trying to unload old 9-pin dot matrix printers now. If that's all you can afford, it's better than no printer at all. But ink jet printers and laser printers are getting less expensive all the time, and the quality is far greater.

• Add a graphics program. This will enable you to create a logo. Then every time you print out a letter or invoice you add the logo. It definitely adds a degree of professionalism. Also, you can create your own business cards, letterhead, and display ads.

Which leads us to another step you can take now—adult education classes. A beginning accounting class or word processing class will do wonders for your confidence. These classes are fun, low-key, inexpensive, and you may meet other people pursuing opportunities similar to the ones you are considering. They can be a great source of information and inspiration.

A good used computer/printer combination will cost about $500.00. A new computer with all the latest bells and whistles will cost $2000 or more. You will also need to allow a few dollars for other related items.

Scanner

This is definitely a luxury item. Even a used scanner will run hundreds of dollars, and they require that you have accompanying software, which can take up a lot of memory.

The advantage to a home inspector having a scanner is that you can scan in sections of the house layout to include in your final report and then add type and arrows to show exactly where a problem area is located. You can also scan in that photo of the house that you took for your office wall and add that to your report for artistic appeal.

While these things might seem unnecessary, remember, clients are just looking for a reason to use one professional instead of another. Give them every reason you can think of to use you and you will be very very busy!

Modem

Like the scanner, a modem may be a luxury item for this particular career, but there are a few advantages. For one thing if you hook up to an online service like CompuServe or Prodigy, you will find, no doubt, other home inspectors to converse with via e-mail. This can be fun and can be enlightening. For instance if you suddenly pick up a client with a really old house and you are not sure of some of the peculiarities that you should look for, going online gives you access to thousands of professionals all over the world.

Again, a class or demonstration from an online company will give you an quick insight into the world of cyberspace. Most new computers come with built-in modems. If you buy a used computer, a modem will cost between $50-$300 depending on how fast a modem you buy. Older modems are slow, but unless you are downloading complex graphics files, should be just fine for starting out.

Other things you will need include a desk ($50-$150), a filing cabinet ($50-$100), business cards, letterhead, envelopes ($25-$200, depending on quantity), a day planner or at least a professional-looking notebook for meetings ($10-$50), a briefcase or portfolio ($50-$200), and various miscellaneous office supplies like pens, pencils, calculator, computer discs, etc. ($50).

As you can see, you will need to invest some money to get started. The amount varies according to how much of the above listed equipment you already have or can borrow or rent. The important thing is to look professional immediately. You do not want to lose a great opportunity because you look like this is the first time you have ever done this sort of thing—even if it is!

Figuring Costs

Having decided that you are ready and able to accept the challenge of starting your own business, it is necessary to take a look at your overall financial picture. Even if you have a healthy savings account, or feel you can start your business with a minimal capital investment, diagnosing your personal financial situation will help you determine on-going expenses.

The easiest way to estimate exactly how much money you will need to get your business started and to cover expenses, including personal living expenses, for the first six months is to prepare a *Cost of Living* or *Cash Flow Statement* and a *Projected Expense Chart*. Samples are provided on the following pages for your use.

Preparing the *Projected Expense Chart* will give you a fairly accurate picture of what it will cost to open the doors and indicate how much income you must generate to realize a profit. The other advantage of creating these charts early in the game is that when you do find that you want to explore funding options, you will already have two of the required documents prepared and will only need to update them.

Your first step is to ask yourself the following questions:

a) Do I generally pay my bills on time or wait until my creditors start sending me collection notices?

b) Have I regularly reconciled my bank statement so I know how much money I have in my checking account at any given time?

c) Is my philosophy "If I've got it, I spend it" or do I typically carefully plan how I am going to use my income?

d) Have I ever developed a personal budget so I know how much money is coming in, how much is going out and what I have left over?

These are important aspects of your financial personality that will be helpful to understand when running your business. As your business and subsequent involvement with financial matters grows, it will be vital that you have a handle on your philosophy about money. And there is no time like in the beginning, when your business concept is being formed, to start learning.

The Cash Flow Statement

Using the chart on page 73, you can determine your personal living expenses for the past three to six months to help you gauge what you will need to survive during the early stages of your business.

The easiest way to complete the statement is to use your checkbook register, if you write checks for most purchases, and/or cash receipts and copies of money orders as research tools. If your expenses are relatively consistent from month to month, you should be able to get an overview by analyzing one month. A more accurate picture will emerge if you break down income and expense for three to six months to account for periodic payments, such as taxes, insurance and seasonal spending.

Using the samples provided, fill in the amounts in each category from your checkbook register or receipts. Use a separate sheet for every month that you are analyzing. For miscellaneous spending, a standard calculation is 5% of monthly income. Add up each month's expenses, total them all and then divide that figure by the number of months you are analyzing. This will give you an average month expense figure.

Follow the same procedure for income. You can then subtract your expenses from your income to see where you stand. If you have computed your figures accurately, you might run across a few surprises. It isn't unusual to discover that we spend more money than we realize, often on miscellaneous, unneeded purchases. You may be able to see some areas where you can cut back.

The main point, however, is that you now know a) how much or whether you can afford to invest your own money in your new business and b) what it costs you to live comfortably, which will help you set income goals for the business.

Cash Flow Statement
Month Of _____

Income		Expenses	
Wages	$_____	Rent or mortgage	$_____
Miscellaneous	_____	Auto loan	_____
		Gas & car repairs	_____
		Auto insurance	_____
TOTAL	$_____	Life insurance	_____
		Medical insurance	_____
		Homeowners insurance	_____
		Taxes	_____
Savings	$_____	Loan payments	_____
		Food: At home	_____
Credit Line	$_____	Food: Dining out	_____
		Telephone	_____
Home Equity	$_____	Utilities	_____
		Household repairs, etc.	_____
		Medical bills	_____
		Credit card payments	_____
		Interest expense	_____
		Clothing/dry cleaning	_____
		Travel	_____
		Miscellaneous	_____
		Savings	_____
		TOTAL	$_____

Start-up Costs

Every business owner has specific standards about how they want to run their operation. One person may feel perfectly comfortable waiting until they are making a profit to order business cards. Another wouldn't dream of opening the doors without cards, brochures and letterhead already printed.

You will have your own ideas about what you need before opening your business. Then, you must find out what it will cost and, if at all possible, prepare the Start-Up Statement as outlined in this section.

It is also advisable to figure how much it will cost to run the business for three to six months, using the sample Projected Expense Forecast which follows. A six month projection should give you the opportunity to start getting an idea of your profits down the line.

Preparing the Start-Up Statement and Projected Expense Forecast involves conducting some research. For example, to estimate the cost of business cards or letterhead stationery, contact several printers or copy shops in your area and obtain quotes. Call the local newspaper for prices on different types of ads, including display and classified. An insurance agent will be able to give you an estimate on liability coverage. Check with the telephone company for information and rates on installing a phone line. You can also start to shop around to find the best prices on office supplies, equipment and materials needed to conduct business.

After completing your research, incorporate the information on the blank charts. Some of your figures, such as those for telephone expenses, will be "guesstimated." But the final figure will give you a good idea of start up and operational costs for the first six months.

Start-Up Costs

Furniture:	Purchase price	$_____	
	Down payment required		$ _____
Fixtures:	Purchase price	$_____	
	Down payment required		$ _____
Equipment:	Purchase price	$_____	
	Down payment required		$ _____

Installation and deliver costs _____

Decorating & leasehold improvements _____

Deposits: Utilities and rent _____

Fees: Legal, accounting, consulting, etc. _____

Licenses & permits _____

Starting inventory _____

Supplies _____

Printing _____

Pre-opening advertising & promotion _____

Miscellaneous: _____

Total Start-Up Expense $ _____

Less: Available Start-Up Capital (minus) $ _____

Total Amount Needed $ _____

Projected Expense Statement

Months:	1st	2nd	3rd	4th	5th	6th
Rent						
Utilities						
Telephone						
Insurance						
Professional Services						
Taxes & Licenses						
Advertising						
Office Supplies						
Office Equipment						
Inventory						
Business auto expense						
Travel expense						
Entertainment						
Dues & subscriptions						
Salaries						
Owner's draw						
Loan payments						
Interest payments						
Miscellaneous						
TOTALS						

Have this sample chart enlarged at your local copy shop if planning to use it as part of your Business Plan. Enlarging it will cost you a few cents, but can save you many dollars in the long run, because of the increased awareness of your financial picture.

Utilizing the same theory, you can develop a Projected Income Statement, drawing from industry figures available through your trade association or other research sources.

This would include all income realized from cash sales, collection on outstanding invoices, credit card sales and miscellaneous income. By subtracting your total expenses from total income, you will get a clear picture of projected profit or loss.

All of these statements will be requested by loan officers, venture capitalists and the Small Business Administration (SBA) if and when you apply for a loan. They require this kind of paperwork to ensure that you have basic business knowledge and a commendable track record, and are serious about your venture. You will also be required to fill out a personal financial statement, available through the lending institution, especially if you are the sole owner or a general partner in the business.

Start-Up Expenses

Low-End Start-Up
  (Home-Based Operation)

Start-Up Marketing	$400.00
Office Supplies/Equipment	60.00
Insurance (monthly)	20.00
Licenses/Filing Fees	40.00
Total Investment	**$520.00**

Average Investment
  (Commercial Location)

Office Furniture	300.00
Business Licenses	20.00
Fictitious Name Statement (FNS)	10.00
Publishing FNS	40.00
Business Telephone Installation	150.00
Answering Machine	50.00
Fax Machine	300.00
Insurance (monthly)	40.00
Start-Up Marketing	1,000.00
Total investment	**$1,910.00**

*These prices are general averages and will vary according to region.

8

BASIC REQUIREMENTS: EQUIPMENT & SUPPLIES

Home Inspection Equipment

There are a few specialty items that you will need in order to do a thorough job. Fortunately, many of the items you will need are everyday items that you probably already own. Prices are based on local purchases or catalog purchases.

• **Tape Measure**—You will use this to measure distances between studs, check the width of porch beams and joists to make sure they are up to code, measure door heights and even driveway lengths. A good, 25-foot tape measure will run about $20-$25.

• **Hammer**—You can learn many things by tapping. For instance, tapping a basement floor with a hammer can help you determine if it is thick enough or has pockets where underground water might build up leading to permanent dampness. If tapping reveals a hollow sound, this may be an indication that the floor is a problem. A Hammer will cost $8-$10.

• **Level and Square**—The human brain oftentimes tries to straighten things up for us. A simple level and carpenter's square can check patios, floors, door jams, windows, and many other things for construction quality and house settling. Levels can be purchased for $10 or less, squares are $5-$10.

• **Rubber Ball or Marble**—This is another easy way to test for levelness of counters, floors, etc. Also an excellent way to check for drainage on roofs and porches—where the ball rolls, so will the water. Cost $2 or less.

• **Plumb Bob**—All houses settle. Out-of-plumb houses will settle unevenly. This is usually a sign of a poorly built house. This is known to some in the industry as a Walk-Away Factor. If the house has out-of-plumb walls and roof line—potential buyers should walk away from the deal!

• **Stud Finder**—Especially in older homes, studs may not be as close together and the nails holding the wallboards may be sparse. Studs should be 16 inches apart, and nails usually 6-8 inches apart holding the wallboard. A simple stud finder can be purchased for about $5, but a better, electronic model can be had for about $40.

• **Screwdriver**—One use for your plastic handle screwdriver will be to check for dry rot on fence posts and any other wood supports that come into contact with the ground. Simply stabbing a fence post at ground level will determine the extent of damage. With a jabbing motion see how far the screwdriver indents into the post. If it goes in easily, there is extensive damage and the posts must be replaced.

• **Flashlight**—Crawl spaces, chimneys, inside furnaces, behind water heaters, you name it, there are numerous dark places to inspect. Get a powerful enough plastic flashlight that will survive being dropped. Cost $10-$20.

• **Telescoping Mirror**—You will use this to look under water heaters, inside furnaces, behind things, etc. Available at most specialty hardware stores for $5-$10.

• **Binoculars**—A pair of binoculars enables you to see most, if not all, of the things you need to check on the roof. Remember, you do not have to be exact. If the chimney appears to be leaning, you merely note on your report that it should be looked at immediately by a professional contractor. Or, if you are a contractor, you can do a rough cost estimate for replacing a chimney. Binoculars run from $20-$50.

• **Electrical tester**—A simple two-wire electrical tester can be used to make sure outlets are "hot" and properly grounded. Newer homes have three prong receptacles made for grounded plugs. Older homes with two prong receptacles should also be properly grounded and can accept adapters. To check these, put one lead wire from your tester on the screw that holds the cover plate on. Place the other lead in one receptacle, then the other. One of them should light the bulb. If not, the outlet is not working or is not properly grounded. You can also test grounding by placing one lead of a multitester on a faucet with the other lead in the grounding receptacle. The needle should not move. Simple testers are available for under five dollars at almost any hardware store. Multitesters may be slightly higher.

• **Water Pressure Gauge**—Available at most plumbing supply houses, this tool will help you quickly determine water pressure. Without the tool, turn on all the water outlets at once and see how badly pressure drops. If some faucets almost stop completely, there is not enough water pressure and a new pump may be required. A good gauge will cost $12-$15.

• **Radon Gas Tester**—There has been a lot of concern about radon gas, which is the product of uranium breaking up down deep in the earth. It is odorless, colorless and—deadly! Some specialty hardware stores now carry radon gas testers. If you can't find one try contacting the department of physics at your local university or the local Environmental Protection Agency. Cost is about $10.

• **Gas Leak Detector/Carbon Monoxide Detector**— This tool will help you pinpoint a leak. Without the tool, simply write on your report that there was evidence of gas and that the clients should call an expert.

• **You will also need** a supply of pens or pencils, a good pair of rubber-soled shoes or boots, and a set of clothing that you know will get dirty. A towel is also handy for wiping your hands. A jackknife can also be useful for scraping.

Computer System

One of your basic needs will be a good word processor, enabling you to easily perform a wide variety of tasks from marketing to billing.

Computer prices are dropping rapidly, and you can currently buy a perfectly good used system for under $500; check the classifieds of local publications. If you wish to have the latest and greatest, expect to pay $1,500 to $3,000 for it. If you have the time to shop around, you can purchase a good computer system for between $700 and $1,500. Also, look for new-merchandise bargains at grand openings of computer stores, year-end closeouts, etc.

Frequently, the computer you purchase will come equipped with word processing and other proprietary software packages, so shop around for the best deal.

Software

There are a number of software packages well-suited to a home inspection operation. However, you don't necessarily need an industry-specific software package, as long as the business software package you choose has the following: accounting; the ability to link to other software systems; word processing; report generation; and a graphics capability.

When choosing a software package, begin by analyzing all the essential elements: everything from data processing to accounting. Then contact computer stores and software manufacturers for information, brochures, etc. Make sure the software is compatible with your hardware if you already own a computer; otherwise, tailor the hardware to the best software package(s).

Arrange for a software demonstration, and bring along your list of requirements. If you're not computer-literate, bring along someone who is, and during the demonstration be sure to use the equipment yourself, making sure it's user-friendly.

Most important, compare each software system with your needs, not the features of other systems. You ultimately are the one who has to use the program and be satisfied with it. If it costs hundreds of dollars and has a lot of bells and whistles you'll never need or use, keep looking. Shop carefully and base your choice on your own business projections and the market you'll be serving. One alternative is to buy an integrated package—one combining several applications (word processing, accounting, database management, and so on).

The leading packages in all software categories are too numerous to outline here. What follows is a glance at the proven winners and most commonly used programs (most are available both for IBM-compatibles and Macintosh): spreadsheet/accounting (Lotus 1-2-3, Excel); database management (Paradox, dBASE, Quattro Pro); word processing (WordPerfect, Microsoft Word); graphics (CorelDraw!, QuickDraw); and integrated software (Microsoft Works is generally considered one of the best available).

Printers

Printers are broken down into three categories: laser (essential for high-quality graphic and desktop publishing applications), dot-matrix (still the biggest seller, and acceptable for a range of applications from correspondence to billing), and ink-jet (used for graphic and business applications).

Laser. Hewlett-Packard dominates much of the laser market with its LaserJet series. Ask your computer dealer for the lowest-cost LaserJet (at this writing Hewlett-Packard makes a good low-cost alternative perfect for the home office). Also consider low-cost offerings from

Okidata.

Dot-matrix. Popular choices here include printers from Epson, Panasonic, Okidata, and Microline. If you don't have a need for high-quality graphic output, and plan to use your computer for correspondence and accounts payable/receivable, dot-matrix printers are the low-cost way to go.

Ink jet. Again, the leader in this category is Hewlett-Packard with a popular DeskJet series that comes in both black-and-white and color models.

Modems

Modems transmit and receive computer data over telephone lines, connecting the home or office-based business with the outside world, from a print shop down the street to a client in Europe.

Modems usually are categorized by their transmission (or baud) rate, measured in bits (or characters) per second. Baud rates are typically 300, 1200, and 2400, but more commonly are upwards of 9600. Modems 1200 baud and higher are recommended for long documents. The higher the baud rate, the faster the transmission time and thus the lower your phone bill, since transmission time is billed in the same manner as a phone call. A recent addition to the modem family is the fax modem, turning your phone into an all-purpose retrieval/transmission center.

Notebooks

These lightweight, battery-powered laptops can be used as stand alone systems or as add-ons to your home computer, in both cases providing system access at remote locations—from the back seat of a limo or a 747 at 30,000 feet. They're more costly than their more conventional counterparts (upwards of $2,500), but can be worth the expense if you frequently need computer access at a variety of locations.

CD-ROMs

The storage medium of the future has not only arrived, it's standard equipment on a number of computer systems, enabling users to store 150,000 pages of text per disc and take a massive load off their hard drives. CD-ROMs store everything from downloaded fonts to 60-million-word dictionaries, and represent the 21st century's ultimate interactive resource. They'll eventually replace conventional newspapers and libraries, becoming the central link in home information systems.

Fax Machines

Fax machines have become standard equipment in commercial offices and increasingly in the home office, allowing local or worldwide transmission of information in a matter of seconds.

Fax machines come in a variety of sizes, from affordable compact models (recommended for the small business) to larger floor-standing units. Some models are also combination answering machines and flatbed copiers. Some of the higher-end systems use laser printer technology well suited to graphics-oriented data.

Some of the smaller units are now available new for about $275 (shop carefully) and can be bought on the used market for considerably less. Leading manufacturers include Canon, Xerox, and Sharp.

Furniture and Supplies

You will need basic office furniture when expanding your business. Whenever possible buy used furniture. A desk for general marketing and billing is, of course, essential. But if you plan on computerizing, you'll also need a computer desk with room for a printer and modem. You'll also need shelving for computer disks, books, and other miscellaneous items.

Consider the benefits of a good calculator with tape for billing and record keeping and shelves for storing a library of reference books and other relevant publications. You'll also need such standard supplies as card files, file cabinets, and staplers. In addition, you'll need letterhead stationery, business cards, printed envelopes, and brochures that explain your service.

All are available at local stationers and office supply stores. For record keeping, you'll need index cards, large manila envelopes, files, and invoice forms. Even with a computer storing a lot of your data, these items are still necessary.

Check for wholesale distributors in your area or ask other business people for good suppliers. Get estimates from two or three suppliers before making a final decision. Business supplies can be obtained from mail order companies as well.

Buy or Lease? Making the Choice

You can buy new or used equipment from dealers and independent sellers. Or, if you don't mind rummaging through other people's lives, you can find incredible bargains on supplies and equipment at garage sales, swap meets, thrift shops run by charitable organizations or auctions. Often, it is well worth the time involved because the savings can be tremendous.

Before investing money, do your homework. Talk with other business owners to find out which brand of equipment they use and why they prefer it over other choices on the market. This will help you make the best decision based on your needs and budget.

Also, talk with independent dealers who carry a broad

line of similar types of equipment. They can give you insights on maintenance, longevity, service contracts and prices.

They will also be able to tell you when to expect a drop in price for the item you are interested in, although you can count on seeing sales on major equipment such as computers and other big-ticket items at store openings and during special sales.

Cash or Credit?

Unless you are planning to pay cash for an equipment purchase, you will either make a down payment and set up a payment schedule with the dealer or take out a loan with the bank. With interest rates for bank loans currently running at about 9-12%, you might be able to find a dealer who is willing to handle the financing at a lower rate.

Although this method is a less effective way of establishing creditworthiness, it will serve to get the business going. Another advantage is that if you should find yourself in a tight cash flow situation at any time, a private dealer/lender with whom you have a personal relationship is much more likely to be flexible . . . without charging you a penalty for late payment.

Buying Used Equipment

When buying used equipment from a dealer, the chances of it being in working condition are generally pretty good. Dealers have a reputation to uphold and will stand behind their merchandise, especially if they are firmly established in the community. There are, however, several ways you can scout around to ensure that the one you decide to work with is reputable:

• Find a store with membership in the local chamber of commerce. Although this is not an iron-clad guarantee, it does indicate the store ownership's interest in following business standards established within the community.

• If the dealer also sells new equipment, it is highly likely that much of the used equipment has been traded in by people who are upgrading. You may be able to get an excellent bargain on an item which has been well maintained by the former owner.

• If there is a service department on the premises, you can be assured that used equipment has been reconditioned before being put on sale. It also increases your chances of getting fast, inexpensive and reliable service if needed at a later date.

• Used equipment dealers realize that it is not always easy to find a buyer and should be willing to work with you. Shopping around will give you an idea of average prices and will give you the information you need to negotiate. If the dealer won't work with you, keep looking.

• What are the terms of the warranty? Even used equipment should be covered for a short time for parts and labor, especially if it has been overhauled or reconditioned.

• Is the dealer willing to agree to offer a trade-in allowance on the item you are buying when you decide to upgrade? Of course, there will be stipulations based on wear and tear and time; however, he or she should be willing to consider it.

Buyer Beware

There are other ways to find and buy used equipment, but it falls into the realm of "Buyer Beware." If you choose to deal with private parties through the classified ads or with auctioneers selling off the inventory of a bankrupt business, you must be willing to take a chance. Although the prices will be easy on your budget, the cost of repairing a malfunctioning machine could result in a long-term drain on your profits.

This is not to say that there aren't bargains out there.

In many cases, you will stumble across an incredible deal on a "like-new" computer, as an example. The secret is to know what you are looking for and to have a good idea of how it should work. Do your research by visiting with reliable used equipment dealers before you start looking.

When talking with a private party, ask them how long they have owned the equipment, why they are selling it and if they have kept any repair bills that you can see. Trust your intuition in this kind of situation; if the person seems truly interested in providing you with as much information as possible, chances are the equipment is everything they say it is or isn't. If they tell you it needs a new part, for example, find out what the replacement part costs and ask if they would deduct it from the selling price.

When you go to see the equipment, make sure it runs. Test it out if possible, measure it to make sure it will fit into the space you have available and decide whether you can move it yourself or will have to arrange transportation. Before buying it, try to find out whether there is a servicing outlet nearby or if you must send away for parts, which can be time-consuming and costly, especially when it comes to older models.

Occasionally you will run across an individual who is making payments on a piece of equipment still under warranty. This can be a great deal for you since they will probably accept a small amount of cash and let you take over the payments. Be sure to transfer ownership in writing to prevent complications if you need service under the warranty.

Auctions

Auctions are an excellent way to get good bargains. Watch the business and classified sections of the newspaper for ads about upcoming auctions. The ad will include dates, the reason for the auction (liquidation or bankruptcy), location, time and a partial list of items. In most cases, there will be a preview, enabling potential buyers to view the merchandise before the bidding begins.

By all means, take advantage of the preview to inspect and select equipment you want to bid on. A fee will be required for a bidder registration number, which is held up when you make a bid so the auctioneer's spotters know who has purchased a particular item.

The two rules to remember at auctions are: a) cash or a personal check for the full purchase amount must be paid on the day of the auction and b) don't move your hands or make significant gestures during bidding or you might find that you have purchased something you didn't want.

Leasing Equipment

Leasing is defined as a long-term agreement between two parties for the use of a specific item. The person who leases is known as the lessee, while the owner of the item is referred to as the lessor. Despite the fact that you do not own the equipment when you lease and so can not take advantage of depreciation on it for tax purposes, there are still many benefits for the beginning business owners.

Leasing lets you try out a piece of equipment for a given period of time to determine if it is the best product for your needs. Although you are locked into the terms of the lease, most lessors are flexible.

Know What You Need

Of course, the way to prevent this in the first place is to be absolutely clear about what you expect the equipment to do for you. The service representative from the leasing company is well-versed in tailoring equipment to customer, so do not hesitate to ask questions about capabilities.

Most lessors offer good maintenance contracts as they

want to protect their equipment. Check to see what parts and/or labor are covered before signing the lease. The lessor should also be willing to provide technical advice at no charge, may be willing to offer installation and set-up of the equipment and also provide training, if required.

Payments can be arranged to fit your budgetary needs on a monthly, semi-annual or annual basis. This gives you the freedom to schedule payments for peak cash-flow periods. You can also negotiate the rates and length of time of the lease to keep monthly operating expenses at a minimum.

Conditional Sales Agreement

Under the provisions of a conditional sales agreement, you become the owner of the leased goods from the agreement date. At the end of the lease period, you are required to purchase the item for a pre-established price. This is often referred to as a balloon payment and should be agreed upon by you and the lessor prior to your signing the lease.

The conditional sales agreement, unlike most other leasing contracts, gives you the tax advantage of claiming depreciation on equipment. Depreciation refers to the decrease in the value of an asset because of wear and tear over a period of time.

You are entitled to deduct depreciation, based on value when new, the estimated life of the item and the value at the end of that estimated life, from your income tax. It is best to work with your accountant on determining depreciation of fixed assets.

There is seldom a down payment, other than the first month's lease amount, required on a leased item, since leasing is generally 100 percent financed for the terms of the agreement. This frees your start-up or working capital for other uses.

True Lease Agreements

You can write off lease payments on your income tax, but only if you have a true lease contract. Under a true lease, the lessor owns the equipment at all times during the contract period. If you decided, at the end of the lease, that you wanted to buy the equipment, you would have to pay whatever purchase price was decided by the lessor.

Financial Lease

The financial lease covers a period that does not extend beyond the estimated life of the equipment. Payments must be made as stipulated on the date due and through to the end of the lease. It usually puts the responsibility and cost of maintenance on the lessee.

Operating Lease

The operating lease generally requires the lessor to handle maintenance of the equipment. It offers the option of cancelling the lease, but only if a cancellation clause has been included at the negotiating stage.

The most important aspects of leasing are the terms outlined in the formal lease. Have the lessor draw up a proposal for you, based on everything you have discussed in an initial meeting. If you have any trouble understanding the terms of the proposal, have your attorney review it with you. In fact, it is a definite advantage to have the final lease agreement checked by your attorney or accountant before you sign it.

What Your Lease Agreement Should Include

- The length of the contract in months or years.
- The rate you are to be charged, which is usually a percentage of the total purchase price computed on a monthly rate.
- Your payment schedule.
- Purchase option, if applicable, at the end of the lease.
- Renewal option, if applicable, which allows you to carry the lease over for an additional period of time.
- Cancellation agreement in the event you want or need to cancel the lease.
- Maintenance stipulations (who pays for parts & labor).
- Substitution options if updated equipment is introduced and you want to take advantage of improvements.
- Any provisions particular to the lease, including tax allowances for depreciation, insurance liability in case of loss or damage and your responsibilities in reporting a move or other major change.

Whether you decide to borrow, buy new equipment, find good used equipment or lease, be sure to get exactly what you need to keep costs at a minimum. This is especially important during the early stages of your business when cash is bound to be tight. You can always upgrade or add to your equipment inventory as profits increase.

9

SELECTING PROFESSIONALS

From the start-up stage and as your business continues to grow and prosper, you will need the assistance of several professionals, including a lawyer, an accountant and an insurance agent.

The best way to find a professional is, according to the majority of business owners, through personal recommendations from other entrepreneurs, especially those in similar businesses as yours, and from friends or relatives. The most important factor is that the person doing the recommending understands exactly what you will need from the professional you will be hiring.

For example, your cousin's divorce lawyer is probably not as well suited to helping you draw up a partnership agreement as the attorney a friend used to help them incorporate their business.

Before making a decision, talk to several recommended professionals until you find someone who can best satisfy your needs for the business as outlined below and who has a fee structure you can afford. Equally important is that it is someone whom you feel comfortable with, especially during those times when you are forced by external forces to call five times a week to resolve a problem or complete a specific task. In many cases, because attorneys and accountants often work on a particular business matter in conjunction with one another, the attorney you select may be able to suggest an accountant who can properly service your business, or vice versa.

If you are planning to hire an attorney or an accountant, you should start "interviewing" likely candidates eight to nine months prior to the date you plan to start the business. This will give you time to find a suitable match and give them time to take care of all pre-startup functions, such as establishing your business form and helping you with your business plan.

What to Expect from Professional Services

Legal

You need an attorney with broad-based expertise in business who can help you with such matters as raising capital, legal and tax ramifications and the benefits of various business forms including sole proprietorship, partnership or corporation. Also important are name clearance (to ensure that you are not using a name already designated by another company), legal tips on operating in your desired location, and the ability to file all necessary legal papers and documents needed for financing and establishing your business.

He or she will review contracts and lease agreements, and can provide support with collection problems. The lawyer you select should also be willing and able to represent you in the event of any claims that are brought against you or lawsuits you initiate.

Fees

Depending on your lawyer's expertise, reputation and where he/she is located (metropolitan area versus small town, for example), fees will differ dramatically. In a smaller community, lawyers often charge a set rate for the job being done while "city" lawyers typically charge by the hour with fees ranging anywhere from $65 to $250 per hour.

This does not include the extraneous expenses involved, such as the $300 to $1,000 cost of incorporating, depending on the state you operate in. Fees also do not include supplemental costs, such as travel and telephone, incurred by the attorney in the handling of your case.

A good way to get an idea of what to expect in the way of fees in your area is to check with your local chamber of commerce or the state bar association, generally located in the capital city. The bar association may also be able to provide you with information about a particular attorney's reputation and expertise.

When talking with potential attorneys—and when you have found one who is compatible to your needs—always be sure to ask for an outline of expenses and also find out if they are willing to notify you when the fees for a particular job will be exceeded.

Accounting

The accountant you select should, early on, be able to work with you on putting together your business plan, including your projected profit and loss statements, for financing.

Down the line as your business is being established, the accountant will help you set up your books and, once in operation, should handle your tax returns, prepare financial statements and offer financial advice regarding tax matters, cash flow, investments to maximize the use of profits and the tax regulations regarding employees, when you are ready to hire.

Fees

As with attorneys, there is a professional association in your state capital which certifies and maintains records on the reputation and fee structures of accountants. The basis for fee structuring does vary slightly, however, with accountants. Some charge by the hour, others by the day and still others work on a set monthly retainer, based on the estimated amount of time they will be required to spend on your work. Hourly fees, however, average between $25 and $100 depending on expertise and location.

Insurance

Before setting out on your search for an insurance agent, it is advisable to have already established your business form and learned exactly what insurance the law in your area requires you to carry (fire, liability, etc.) And if you will be hiring employees, find out what kind of program you want to offer, as well as what you will need for your own medical and life insurance.

The insurance agent you choose should be familiar with the needs of businesses and business owners, not just the standard life and disability policies. Your insurance needs will change as your business grows and expands (i.e., employee health, workman's compensation, etc.). At that point, you may want to consider key person coverage to insure that a small company can survive if a major partner or employee dies.

There are also a number of pension programs and stock-option programs available in the event you want to offer employees the incentive to increase their participation in the company in exchange for partial "ownership" down the line.

Fees

The fees for your agent's expertise are paid from your premiums, and there should definitely not be any extra charge to you for advice or administration of your insurance policies and programs.

10

TAXES, LICENSES AND PERMITS

As a business owner, you are responsible for the timely report filing and payment of federal, state and local taxes. Whether you have an accountant prepare your returns, or do it yourself, the task will be made much easier if you establish a systematic record-keeping system and keep your records accurate and up-to-date.

This includes maintaining all written documents pertaining to the financial aspect of your business; invoices, bank statements, receipts of any and all business expenses and deposit slips.

One of the easiest ways to keep control of the "paper dragon" is to set up a 9 x 12 inch manila envelope or a file folder for each of the following categories: Paid Bills—both personal and business; Sales Receipts of every product you've sold or service job performed; Inventory records based on on-going inventory control and quarterly audits; Copies of Invoices or billing statements that are paid with a separate file for those still due you; Receipts for miscellaneous cash purchases; Auto and Entertainment receipts from travel and promotional activities.

All of these documents must be kept for at least five years to substantiate deductions claimed on your income tax returns in the event of an I.R.S. audit. Make up new file folders or envelopes at the beginning of each year and store the old ones in a safe place.

It is not only a time-consuming task that can take you away from the important job of running your business, but preparing income tax returns, especially for the federal government, has become almost an art form. Tax law is a constantly changing, complicated fact of life. It is strongly recommended that you have an accountant lined up to prepare your taxes and keep you informed of any pertinent changes during the year.

Business Deductions

The deductions that you will most likely qualify for as a business owner include expenses incurred for the operating of business, such as telephone, postage, advertising, bank service charges, travel and expense of conventions, interest, dues to professional organizations and subscriptions to magazines pertaining to your business, among others.

If you have established your business at home, you will be able to deduct that portion of the house used exclusively for business, as well as a percentage of your costs for telephone service and utilities.

Again, because of the complexity and obscurity of many of the deductions, it is best to have a professional do your taxes to ensure you get the full benefits you are entitled to.

This list provides an overview of the tax returns which may be applicable to your business situation. It is meant only to inform you. Filing requirements will be determined by the type of business, the legal structure (sole proprietorship, partnership or corporation), income from the business, your location, state and local laws and whether or not you have employees.

For example, as the sole proprietor of your business you would probably only be required to file personal federal and state returns based on profit or loss with the appropriate schedules for business expenses, pay sales, self-employment and estimated taxes, local business license fees and sales tax.

Federal Tax Returns

Form 1040: Income tax for Sole Proprietors, Partners or
    S Corporation shareholders.
Schedule C: Profit (or Loss) from Business or Profession.
Form 1065: Partnership income tax return.
Schedule K-1: Partner's share of Income, Credits, Deductions, etc.
Form 1120: Corporation tax return with applicable support schedules.
Form 2553: S Corporation Filing
Form 1120-S: S Corporation Tax Return
Form 1040ES: Quarterly Estimated Tax for Sole Owner or Partner.
Form 1120W: Quarterly Estimated Tax for Corporation.
Form 940: Federal Unemployment (Social Security) Tax for Sole Owner,
    Partner, Corporations.
Schedule SE: Annual return of self-employment tax for Sole Proprietor
    or Partner.

State Income Tax

Each state has corresponding filing requirements; however, form and schedule numbers vary. Contact your State Franchise Tax Board or your accountant for details.

Local Taxes

Taxes will vary from city to city and county to county; however, you may be required to pay city income tax, local sales tax as well as real or personal property taxes. Check with your local government offices for specifics.

Licenses and Permits

To operate your business, you will need permits and licenses based on the requirements in your area and the type of business you are running. You will probably, however, be required to obtain the following documents no matter where you live.

Local Business License
Basically this is simply a fee paid to the city or county in which you are located which allows you to operate your business in that area. Some cities will also require you to pay a percentage of your gross sales every year.

Fictitious Name Statement

This is a registration for protection of your business name. Filing for the fictitious name statement will also involve a city or county-wide search to make sure you are not duplicating an existing name. See details in "Naming Your Business" in this section.

Seller's Permit or Resale Certificate

Required only if you are going to be charging sales tax. Services are often exempt.

Health Permit

Required only if you are preparing or distributing food in any manner. Involves an initial inspection and sporadic follow-up inspections by health department officials.

Taxpayer Identification Number

Available from the I.R.S. by filing Form SS-4, in the case of partnerships, S corporations or corporations. Sole proprietors are required to have a taxpayer identification number if they pay wages to one or more employee or file pension or excise tax forms.

Your local governmental offices or your attorney will be able to give you information on the specific licenses and permits, and required fees for each as required in your case.

Legal Structure

As a self-employed business owner, you are required to decide on a legal form of business for tax reporting purposes. There are four basic classifications, as outlined below. If, after reviewing them, you are still unsure of which way to go, it would be advisable to talk with a lawyer about the advantages and disadvantages of each structure for your particular business.

Sole Proprietorships

This is the easiest to establish and the preferred structure for many small business owners. A proprietorship is relatively free from government regulation, as the business has no existence apart from the owner. Profits from the operation of business are treated as personal income for purposes of taxation and your proprietary interest ends when you die or dissolve the business.

The major drawback of a proprietorship is that you are personally liable for any and all claims against the business and undertake the risks of the business to the extent of all assets, whether they are used in the business or personally owned. As a sole proprietor, you will be required to file self-employment tax returns and ordinarily would have to make estimated tax payments on a quarterly basis.

General Partnership

This is also easy to set up and administer. Since responsibilities and capitalization are usually shared by two or more partners, taxation is based on each partner's share of business income and determined by their individual tax rates. Again, claims against the business can be filed against personal assets and financial liability is shared equally by all partners.

Limited Partnership

This structure can be established when one or more people are willing to invest cash or tangible property in the business with active participation in the daily operations. However, there must be at least one general partner who carries unlimited financial liability and usually maintains a full-time managerial position within the company.

The limited partner(s) are liable only for business debts up to the amount of their investment. Although a partnership is not a taxable entity, it must figure its profit or loss and file an annual tax return, which also becomes part of the partners' personal returns.

Corporation

In this structure, stock or shares in the business are sold to investors or stockholders, who then control the company. The advantage is that corporate stockholders are removed from any liability against personal assets. The most anyone can lose in the event of bankruptcy or a liable claim is their stock.

The privilege of reduced liability, however, creates paperwork (articles of incorporation and annual reports for the state tax commission and federal regulators); expenses (filing and licensing fees) and double taxation (the corporation is taxed on profits, while stockholders and elected officers are taxed individually on wages and/or dividend income).

Subchapter S Corporation

This structure has proved to be a real boon for small business owners who want the benefit of corporate protection from personal liability without double taxation. In a Subchapter S corporation, a maximum of 35 stockholders (who can be family members) report their share of corporate income on individual tax returns.

The corporation itself is generally exempt from federal income tax; however, it may be required to pay a tax on excess net passive investment income, capital gains or built-in gains. To structure your company as a Subchapter S corporation, all of the shareholders must consent to the choice.

All businesses, regardless of size, are required to maintain detailed records and file the necessary tax returns. In a corporation, regular meetings must be held. The stockholders elect a board of directors, who establish and monitor corporate policy. The board selects corporate officers to conduct the operations of the business.

Sole proprietorships are the most convenient and least complicated form of business organizations for new business owners, especially in the early stages. As your business grows, you will want to explore the options as a way of protecting your personal assets and increasing the potential for expansion capital.

11

NAMING YOUR BUSINESS

As a pet owner, it is unlikely that you would give your German Shepherd a name like Fifi. It wouldn't suit the dog's image, nor would it be appropriate. The same principle applies to choosing a name for your business.

The name you select for your business can be a tremendous asset when it defines the kind of image you want to project. You want the name to attract and appeal to potential customers, to be easily remembered over that of the competition's, and be appropriate to the type of business you are starting.

Today's consumers are constantly bombarded with advertising as they go about their daily routines. Getting their attention, and holding it long enough for them to make an association between your business name and what you are offering, is imperative.

A memorable moniker can mean the difference between continued growth or a mediocre response from an audience victimized by information overload. (It is, of course, important to remember that your ultimate success depends on well designed advertising, careful planning, and quality products and/or service).

Naming Your Home Inspection Business

Take some time to think about this, because your company name needs to fulfill several functions beyond identifying you. The name you choose can affect a customer's perceptions of your legitimacy.

It may serve you best to just use your own name, e.g., Mary's Home Inspection.

Depending on where you live, there may be a number of other Home Inspection businesses with names that are similar to the one you want. Set yourself apart from the flock. Choose a name that is catchy and descriptive, and then come up with a logo that says something about who you are.

Brainstorming

Start by making a list of all the positive aspects of your business that you can think of, and call on friends and relatives to provide as many as they can come up with. Write down all the possibilities, no matter how funny or unusual they seem. A handy tool for business naming is the thesaurus, which will give you a vast number of options for commonplace names. Consider everything that springs forth from your imagination.

When you have created a list of likely candidates, get together with a group of supportive friends and family members and have a brainstorming session to either pick one of the choices you have come up with or to develop something from the ideas listed. Chances are that within a few hours, you will have a name for your business.

Catchy names are fun to design. However, make sure it isn't so offbeat, cute, or trendy as to risk slipping into obscurity as time passes.

The Fictitious Name Statement

You are required to file a fictitious name statement with the county clerk's office where you will be basing the business. While there, you should be able to do a countywide name check on the spot to see if there are any other businesses in the region using the name you have selected. The filing fee depends on where you live, and must be done within thirty days after you officially open your business.

It will also be necessary to publish the fictitious name in a local newspaper; the cost depends on the circulation of the paper. The county clerk's office will advise you about specific requirements in your area.

If you are starting a business that will be operating in a broader market, statewide or nationally, it is important to have your attorney do a name clearance investigation, which can take from three days to three weeks.

Your Visual Image

After you have selected a name that reflects your business image, the next step is translating it into a visual symbol or logo (logo type) to serve as a signature piece for your business. Often this involves creating a visual interpretation of your company name, but in other cases a graphic symbol or trademark is designed to serve as identification.

Some established corporate trademarks are so familiar that you can immediately identify the company even without seeing or hearing its name.

A good example of this includes the logo of the dog with his head cocked to one side. The accompanying copy reads "His Master's Voice," and it's a good bet that you recognize this as the logo for RCA. Another effective logo is the avant-garde apple that identifies Apple computer products.

If you do not have the graphic skills necessary to design a logo with impact, get in touch with your nearest art association (listed in the phone book or available through local art supply shops or galleries) or call a nearby college or university. Ask the head of the art department if your design can be given as a class assignment or if he or she could recommend a student to do the job for a small fee. It will give students practical application, and the design can be used later in their portfolios. You can offer cash or a prize for the best design. The students will undoubtedly meet the challenge with enthusiasm and give you a number of good samples and ideas from which to choose.

Selecting a Typeface

Save sample logos and advertisements that use a typeface you like. Type is an extremely important element of logo design and can also pinpoint the precise image you hope to express. Type not only presents the basic message, it can play a powerful role in the overall appearance of your logo and can actually create atmosphere. A chart of some of the more popular typefaces is included at the end of this chapter.

When deciding on a typeface for your logo, visit print shops or typesetting studios and look at their typeface books. They offer both the usual, functional varieties as well as a selection of unique typefaces that can really dress up your logo and subtly portray a specific personality such as dignified, fun, powerful, classic or cutting edge.

Have the logo and your business information (address, phone number, etc.) set in more than the one typeface so that you can see how they will look when printed. Also ask to have them set in both small (10- to 12-point for business cards) and larger (20- to 40-point for letterhead) versions. Once typeset, you will be able to make a final decision about which typeface suits the image you want to project.

Typesetters generally have a minimum fee based on the amount of time they spend on a job, which can vary from $15 per hour in a small city to $50 per hour in a business area, as high as $100 per hour in major metropolitan areas. That's why it's important to shop around.

Word processing specialists or independent desktop publishers can also provide a variety of typefaces and formats at less expense. Since you will only be having a few words typeset, the time and cost required to set them in several different styles should certainly be affordable.

> *Historically, in developing business names, simplicity has scored the highest points. The name you choose should be short, to the point and easy for consumers to pronounce.*

Business Cards and Stationery

The typeface and logo you eventually choose will be used on your letterhead; in your display and telephone advertising; on all promotional materials, including flyers, brochures, and announcements; on your sign; and on statements and invoices.

They will also be used on your business cards, one of the most inexpensive and convenient ways to inform people about your service or product. Once you have had cards printed, be generous. Give one to everyone you meet and always be sure to carry a supply wherever you go.

Most fast-print copy centers are prepared to help you if you decide not to design your own business cards and stationery. They have samples of business forms, letterheads, and cards with various styles to choose from. Make sure that your company name, logo, address, and phone number are included where necessary. If you have a fax and/or toll-free number, be sure those numbers are included. When someone looks at your card or letterhead, it must tell them instantly who you are, what your business is, and how you can be reached.

Sample Typefaces

Arial
ABCDEFGHIJ
abcdefghij

Benguiat Frisky
ABCDEFGHIJ
abcdefghij

Bookman
ABCDEFGHIJ
abcdefghij

Bookman Bold
ABCDEFGHIJ
abcdefghij

Brush Script
ABCDEFGHIJ
abcdefghij

Chicago
ABCDEFGHIJ
abcdefghij

Eras Book
ABCDEFGHIJ
abcdefghij

Eras Bold
ABCDEFGHIJ
abcdefghij

Fenice
ABCDEFGHIJ
abcdefghij

Fenice Bold
ABCDEFGHIJ
abcdefghij

Futura
ABCDEFGHIJ
abcdefghij

Futura Light
ABCDEFGHIJ
abcdefghij

Futura Heavy
ABCDEFGHIJ
abcdefghij

Futura Extra Bold
ABCDEFGHIJ
abcdefghij

Garamond
ABCDEFGHIJ
abcdefghij

Garamond Bold
ABCDEFGHIJ
abcdefghij

Garamond Bold Italic
ABCDEFGHIJ
abcdefghij

Geneva
ABCDEFGHIJ
abcdefghij

Helvetica
ABCDEFGHIJ
abcdefghij

Helvetica Black
ABCDEFGHIJ
abcdefghij

Helvetica Condensed
ABCDEFGHIJ
abcdefghij

Monaco
ABCDEFGHIJ
abcdefghij

Palatino
ABCDEFGHIJ
abcdefghij

Palatino Italic
ABCDEFGHIJ
abcdefghij

Palatino Bold
ABCDEFGHIJ
abcdefghij

Park Avenue
ABCDEFGHIJ
abcdefghij

Stone Serif
ABCDEFGHIJ
abcdefghij

Stone Serif Italic
ABCDEFGHIJ
abcdefghij

Times Roman
ABCDEFGHIJ
abcdefghij

Times Italic
ABCDEFGHIJ
abcdefghij

Notes

Key Points:

_____

_____

_____

_____

Personal Thoughts:

_____

_____

_____

_____

_____

_____

_____

_____

Additional Research:

_____

_____

_____

_____

12

PREPARING A BUSINESS PLAN

Developing your business plan is the most important process you will undertake in your career as an entrepreneur, regardless of the size or type of business you have decided to start.

A well thought-out business plan will serve as a blueprint while your idea turns into a recognizable entity and as it grows into a stable and profitable venture. Too often we hear former small business owners say they probably could have made a success of their business if they had only known what to expect from the beginning . . . and that is where the business plan comes in.

Too many new entrepreneurs are unfamiliar with the importance of planning or consider themselves an exception and feel they can succeed by winging it or dealing with problems as they arise. Not so!

Every business, whether a large commercial or a small home-based venture, needs to analyze its potential, examine strengths and weaknesses and determine the future of the company. It works for the major corporations and it will work for you, especially once you become involved in the day-to-day operations of the business! Having a business plan will give you the freedom to follow the steps you have carefully laid out with regard to budgeting, the success ratio of a product or service, the hiring of employees and other growth decisions.

Advantages of a Business Plan

Once you have made the all-important decision to leave the 9-to-5 world behind, take the plunge and become a business owner, you must devise a specific statement that clearly outlines what you plan to do, when you plan to do it and how you will accomplish the short and long-term goals.

Not only will this keep you on track, it will serve as an indicator of your sincerity and knowledge to others when you go out to find start-up or expansion capital and as the foundation of your financing proposal.

The other advantage is that the actual task of putting your business plan together will help you define and clarify every step of your concept and, if done in a conscientious and objective manner, will point out potential trouble spots that can be addressed before they become a major problem.

If all the necessary components are covered, it will put your business on the road to profit. It is a sure bet that, down the road, if you find your business is not generating the income you had originally projected, it will very likely be because you didn't include one or more of the basic business plan requirements.

Not a Guessing Game

Like any other major project, preparing a business plan involves time and research. It shouldn't be a guessing game. It will be necessary to ask yourself some very specific questions and to answer them thoughtfully and honestly. The business plan is your foundation, so build it carefully to ensure that it works at optimum efficiency for your needs. And make sure it is typed so you, and others, recognize its importance in the professional scheme of your expanding operation.

An important aspect to remember is that your business plan is not cast in stone. In fact, one of the wonderful things about a business plan is that it invites change and revisions as your business changes. This makes it a companion in your success and, by reviewing it regularly, a partner in your progress.

The best way to approach your business plan is to take paper and pen and devote a few hours to coming up with some hard answers. Putting them down on paper will give you all the information you need to write the plan. Of course, you will want to condense your answers to fit into specific segments within the plan, including (in order of appearance) Concept and Feasibility, Legal Structure, Product or Service, Customer Base, Marketing and Production Goals, Personnel (your resume and Entrepreneurial Profile and those of any other key personnel), and Financial Statements.

It is advisable to start each segment on a separate page and to create a table of contents to place in the front. Be sure it is neatly typed, well-written and organized, and bound in a report folder to preserve it and give it a professional quality, especially when using it as a "sales" tool to convince lenders.

Key Questions to Ask Yourself

The first question you must ask yourself is: Why am I interested in this particular business? Probably to be your own boss and make money ...Independence and Income.

This answer is fine as a personal goal, but it isn't going to be good enough if you are planning to approach potential lenders for funding. They will want to see an overview of your business concept, why you are convinced it will be successful and where it fits in the scheme of similar businesses in your town or city.

> *Show me a person with an obsession about succeeding and a solid business plan and I'll show you a good risk.*
>
> *Anonymous Loan Officer*

The next question you must address is: What is my product or service? This may seem like a ridiculous question since you know your product is gift baskets or your service is catering, local sightseeing tours or whatever, but it goes deeper.

Your written response will include details about the service or a description of your product, preferably positive, and with a focus on why customers will be inclined to purchase from you.

Additional questions to analyze should include:

- Why do I believe there is a need for my product or service?
- How do I plan to develop my business over the next five years?
- How much will I charge to ensure value to the customer and profit for myself?
- Who are my suppliers?

- Who are my customers?
- What equipment do I need to start the business?
- How much inventory and supplies do I need for start-up?
- What will it cost?
- Who is my competition and where are they located?
- What are they offering and how can I improve my offer to attract customers?
- What changes are occurring in my marketing area which will impact my business in the future?
- What are my estimated sales figures for each of the next five years? (A "guesstimate" based on researching similar businesses in the area)
- How will I advertise and promote my business (including estimated costs of doing so)?
- How and where is my product going to be manufactured?
- What is involved in the production—materials, labor, costs?
- Where will my service be performed?
- What equipment is required for my service (costs for leasing versus purchasing)?
- What are other overhead expenses (rent, employees, etc.)?
- How many people will be involved in the business and what are their qualifications?
- If I don't have employees, am I qualified to run the business myself? Will I need outside assistance?

By talking with people in similar businesses, suppliers and direct competitors, as well as your local chamber of commerce, you will gather a great deal of information, both positive and negative, about your potential business. People love to talk about their success and, if you ask the right questions, their failure, as well.

Become an investigative reporter for a few days while preparing to write your business plan and it's guaranteed that you will obtain plenty of good, solid information. A SCORE representative through the Small Business Administration can also offer assistance, or give you resources that will help you develop a realistic business plan.

Trade associations, listed in reference books available at your local library, can provide you with invaluable details on industry facts and figures, such as the percentage of gross sales that should be spent on advertising, the percentage that is typically paid for rent in your particular business and how to price your product or service.

The final item to include in this section of your business plan, when and if presenting it for financing, is a personal résumé, designed to emphasize your business management experience, in general, and your expertise within the area of your chosen business, specifically.

Describe the job duties for every job you have held, including any special aspects that pertain directly to the business. If you cannot prepare the résumé, it is worth the $25 to $40 to have it done professionally.

Financial Statements

Once you have written your overview and description sheets, it is time to get down to numbers. This is the key to your business plan and, unfortunately, the area where many entrepreneurs get bogged down. But without an understanding about the numbers involved, you can never expect to be a good manager and really shouldn't be surprised if you run into money problems within the first year.

Again, utilizing the resources indicated above—chamber of commerce, trade associations, etc.—you will need to work up your financial pages to include the following components, which most lenders will want to see spread out for between one and five years.

• **Projected operating expenses:** Materials, advertising, salaries for employees or outside labor, and other expenses directly related to the cost of doing business.

• **Estimate of gross (before tax) sales revenue:** Based on research figures from trade associations and what the local market dictates, if the business is not yet operating or, if open, how many items or hours of service you plan to sell and the average price.

• **How you arrived at the figures for these statements:** Generally you would base your figures on assumptions made about the number of months of operation, estimated number of sales and the average amount versus the cost of each sale.

• **Cost of equipment and furnishings:** Get estimated quotes, whether planning to purchase or lease these items.

• **Cost of materials for production:** If applicable, or maintenance on equipment needed to run the business.

• **Additional operating expenses:** Rent, telephone and other utilities, business taxes and license fees, office supplies, even decorating costs and a category called "other" to provide a cushion for unexpected expenses.

• **Balance sheet:** Shows assets, such as equipment and operating capital you already have, and liabilities or debts and expenses (if the business has not yet started, this would be a personal balance sheet indicating your net worth; listing all possessions of any value plus cash, stock and other holdings minus all financial responsibilities).

• **Leasehold improvements:** If you are planning to rent a commercial location or redesign a room within your home strictly for business, estimate cleaning and restoration costs in this statement.

By investing the time and energy into this portion of the business plan, you will absorb the numbers into your consciousness and be able to recognize, at a glance, when your costs exceed your profit margin or when you are in a position to start making expansion moves.

If money matters are absolutely beyond your comprehension at this point, it would pay to hire someone to work along with you in developing the financial pages of the plan. There are business consultants and accountants who will probably charge you a substantial amount, or you can approach the accounting or business department of the nearest college and see if there is a qualified student available to help you.

No matter whom you find to assist you, be sure to stay involved in the process . . . the discipline and hard work will guarantee success.

13

THE MATTER OF MONEY: FINANCING ALTERNATIVES

Starting your business without having sufficient capital is setting yourself up for problems from the very beginning. Undercapitalization is cited as one of the major reasons why businesses do not succeed, and this is the result of bad planning.

If you research and record all the goals, marketing data, equipment and supply requirements and financial needs of your venture before actually opening the doors, you will be able to see at a glance how much you need to get going and *why you need it*. That way, there will be no surprises and no reason that your business should suffer from lack of capitalization.

It is important to have the financial resources to cover all your preliminary planning and start-up costs, including expenses incurred to research the feasibility of your business and those required to set up shop, from equipment and supplies to advertising and utility set-up charges. You will also need a surplus to carry you over personally until the business becomes productive. The Cash Flow Statement and Projected Expense Charts provided in Section III will help you determine these expenses.

If, after drawing up your business plan (which is covered in the previous section), you find that your personal resources are not enough to open the business, there are other options available. The four most common methods include: a) starting the business on a part-time basis while holding a full-time job to cover expenses, b) taking on a limited partner, c) going to friends or family members for the money you need or d) applying for a loan through a commercial lender or the Small Business Administration (SBA).

There are, of course, pros and cons to each of these options.

Starting Out Part-time

Starting your business on a part-time or "moonlighting" basis is a decision that must be made based on the nature of the business. If you are planning to capitalize on your skills in upholstering, for example, you should have no trouble building up the business at night and on weekends.

It is perfectly feasible to start small, using your garage or home as your production facility and purchasing an answering machine for potential customers to leave a message while you are at your regular job. When you get home, you simply call them back to discuss prices and arrange a time when it is convenient to pick up the piece of furniture to be upholstered.

On the other hand, if you are planning to start a temporary help agency, for example, it would be in your best interest to go into it on a full-time, dedicated basis, as your potential customers are going to want fast results. They will call someone else if they are even slightly discouraged, such as getting a recorded message when they call.

Starting part-time will be practical in some businesses, but before exploring it as an option you must figure out if your limited availability will affect your credibility, if you really have the time and energy to work at a regular job and try to build a business (not to mention family responsibilities) and whether your ultimate goal is to be self-employed or just to earn a few extra dollars to supplement your base income.

Considering a Partner

Going into business with a limited partner who will put up the money you need while stepping into the background to let you run the business the way you see fit is a feasible idea. You must be sure, however, to have your lawyer draw up a precise partnership agreement that covers every eventuality. Partnerships are typically entered into with the best intentions and the unwavering belief that the business will be successful.

Since this is not always the case—and even if it were— it is a businesslike move to ensure that such aspects as decision making, distribution of profits and losses, contributions of partners and handling disputes and changes are outlined and approved by all the partners.

Friends & Family

The third option, raising capital through friends or family members, is probably one of the most often exercised methods. The advantage of getting a loan from a personal contact is that they know you, undoubtedly trust your ability to make the business go and won't require much in the way of substantiating paperwork, such as complex loan applications, financial statements, etc. In addition, you will most likely be able to negotiate a small interest rate on the loan.

The major disadvantage, according to entrepreneurs who have taken this route, is if the friendly lender decides they want to provide input on the care and maintenance of your business. This problem, however, can be eliminated by a "cards-on-the-table" discussion prior to accepting the loan. In other words, choose your investor carefully!

The second problem has to do with repayment of the loan. Even though you have a loose agreement in writing with your lender, because of friendship or family ties there may come a point when Uncle Bill needs that $10,000 tomorrow to take care of a personal obligation. You can't possibly come up with the money overnight, Uncle Bill gets angry and much of the family turns against you.

> *Money brings some happiness.*
>
> *But, after a certain point, it just brings more money.*
>
> *Neil Simon*

The flip side of the coin is if the business fails and you are unable to pay Uncle Bill or your old college pal the $5,000 he or she put up. These are unpleasant situations, so you must be sure in the beginning to think about the importance of the relationship you have with the potential lender, how the best and the worst of situations would affect the situation and whether you then could justify asking for money.

Commercial Lenders

If you are not able to, or decide against approaching friends or relatives for financial assistance, the next step is a bank, a savings & loan or a credit union. Before approaching any of these commercial lenders you must have carefully developed your business plan, which will include the following documents.

a) a resume or statement outlining your background and capability to operate the business, plus a similar statement about any key employees or partners in the business;

b) a statement of business and personal goals;

c) a description about the business, including research about the market for your product or service;

d) details on how the business is going to be structured (sole proprietorship, partnership, corporation, non-profit status);

e) a projection of profit and loss for a minimum of one year, which forces you to do your homework and investigate how similar businesses in similar locations are doing, and

f) an outline of how much money you need—and why—to keep the business solvent and to support yourself and your family for at least a year.

In addition, you will be required to provide a personal balance sheet which lists your assets, such as property, a car, etc., and liabilities like your mortgage payments, credit card debts, etc., and a credit application which outlines your personal financial history (so they can make a determination on your ability to pay back the loan). The lender will follow through by requesting a credit report from an independent agency, such as TRW, to help them make their decision.

The main thing to remember when applying for a loan with a commercial institution is that lenders aren't as concerned about how much money they loan as they are about how and when they are going to get the money back!

Approaching a Lender

Once you have your business plan and other paperwork prepared, decide which lending institution you want to approach. Certainly, if you have a stable record with a checking or savings account at your regular bank or S&L, that is the place to try first. Set up an appointment with the bank manager or loan officer to make your request and explain why you feel your business venture is worth their investment.

Be aware, however, that banks are more likely to provide you with a loan payable within five or ten years, as opposed to savings & loans, which are more interested in long-term loans, such as for mortgages. Credit unions operate in a similar manner to banks; however, you generally have to be a member. If you do belong to a credit union, it could be your best bet as they offer lower interest rates and can be more flexible in their determinations.

If, for some reason, you do not want to run a loan through your bank, consider talking with other local small

Paying Back the Loan

When you apply for financing, whether through a friend, relative, lending institution, a venture capitalist or some other type of arrangement, the burden of proof as it relates to repayment rests with you.

No one would knowingly grant a loan to an individual or a business that they had doubts about. As a borrower, your responsibility is to show that you will be able to pay back the loan according to the terms agreed to. This can be done through a credit history that demonstrates a sense of responsibility.

business owners. Very often they can steer you to a regional, often independently owned bank or S&L which is empathetic to and supportive of new businesses. In that case, proceed as mentioned above and arrange a meeting with the manager or loan officer.

Present your case in a friendly, yet professional manner. Be realistic and honest about your needs. Do not underbid because of fear that you will not get a loan if you ask for too much. It is always better to start with a higher figure than you actually need so you have a strong negotiating edge.

In addition, most lenders have a pretty good idea about start-up and operating costs of new businesses and are much less likely to give you, and risk losing, a small loan for a business they know calls for more capital. They will be more willing to work with you if you are realistic and obviously knowledgeable about your needs.

If, after your first try, the answer is no, ask for reasons why you are being turned down so you can restructure your presentation. Turn opposition into a learning tool to re-define and polish your material and to develop new negotiating strategies.

There are always other potential lenders you can approach, and the law of averages dictates that you will get your loan if the idea is solid and it is apparent that you have researched the feasibility of starting a business in your particular area.

The SBA

The Small Business Administration (SBA) often goes where no other lender will tread and, as such, is a lender of last resort.

The SBA is a government agency that is well known for providing financing to entrepreneurs who have been repeatedly turned down by commercial lenders (which in fact must be the case before the SBA will consider backing you).

After your loan request with a commercial institution has been denied, you can file an application with the nearest branch of the SBA. It is a good idea to make an appointment with a SCORE (Service Corps of Retired Executives) representative, who volunteers his or her time to the SBA-SCORE program to advise new and established business owners. Your SCORE representative will be able to lead you through the complex paperwork required by the SBA before they make a decision.

In addition, the SCORE volunteers are usually straightforward, knowledgeable men and women who will walk through your business plans with you and offer constructive suggestions. Once the paperwork is completed, a commercial lender will make the loan under the SBA Lender Certification Program, knowing that the government is willing to insure it.

This option is recommended only after you have been turned down by three or more banks, because of the time factor involved in gaining approval and also because of the extensive follow-up reports required of SBA. It is, however, a viable option and one that has helped thousands of dedicated entrepreneurs realize their goals.

Venture Capitalists

Money is available to businesses that are already established and seeking working or expansion capital from groups of investors known as *venture capitalists*. These groups can vary from a few local businessmen with money to invest to major investment companies connected with large corporations or financial organizations.

Venture capital is not like a straightforward business loan. It is usually dependent on a minimum $100,000 investment and, therefore, is not suited to every business situation. Typically, venture capitalists are interested in companies that have a track record, a proven position in the market and a solid growth projection.

But, like a bank or other lending association, venture capitalists want to see a written business plan and a prospectus of future projections. They are looking at your background, the market, the kind of funding you want and your past financial record. Since venture capitalists are looking to earn from 10 to 15 percent on their investment over a relatively short period, they will want to spend a great deal of time talking with you and your associates, customers and suppliers.

Before considering venture capital, we advise discussing it carefully with an attorney who can help you investigate different groups and figure out the best investment structure for you and the organization you choose, and work with their attorney on drawing up an agreement that protects you, since many venture capitalists will want to become a part owner in your company.

This is an option to be considered only when your company is well-established and undergoing rapid growth pains and should be approached with great understanding of the situation.

Other Financing Options

Loan companies are an additional source of funding. However, interest rates are high and they will generally want to have substantial collateral, such as the equity in your house, on record before making a loan.

Insurance companies. Your insurance carrier may be willing to make an investment in your small business, using your insurance policy as collateral. Or, you may even have enough cash value in your policy, depending on the face amount, to provide you with substantial start-up capital.

If this is the case, you will be required to pay only quarterly or semi-annual interest payments on the cash value you have taken out.

Factoring. In this instance, a factoring company "buys" your accounts receivables and advances you a percentage of the full amount due. This is a viable option for well-established service companies that work on a billing basis.

Co-signer. If you have a relative or friend who is already an established business owner or, at least, a home-owner with a solid credit rating, it might be worth your while to ask if they would co-sign on a loan application with you. Although you are still responsible for repayment of the loan, the bank is assured that, in the event you default for any reason, the co-signer will guarantee the obligation. It is often difficult to find someone who will do this, but again it doesn't hurt to ask, especially if it is a last resort option.

Starting Small

Even if you know your particular business is valid and that you have the ability to make it succeed, be certain that your business plan is realistic. If you have chosen to start a business on a grand scale but have minimal capital and little business experience, it may be best to begin a smaller, less elaborate operation at first.

> *The journey of a thousand miles begins with a single step.*
>
> *Chinese Proverb*

You'll require less "seed money" and put yourself in a low-risk position while learning the ropes and seeing if you can handle all the variables of business ownership as it grows.

Smaller businesses have proven to be a great way to learn the successful methods, as well as a vehicle for ironing out the many small details that are often overlooked until you actually start taking care of day-to-day situations. The profits you gain from a smaller venture can be used to expand or invest in bigger business ideas. And, an added bonus is that when you are ready to approach investors or lending institutions, you will be able to show them that you already have a solid track record and a working knowledge of business procedures.

What to Do When Asking for Money

A) *Be sure to ask.* This may seem like a gross statement of the obvious, but you would be amazed at the number of small business owners we talk to who never ask because they are afraid of being turned down.

Unless you are independently wealthy and pursuing your business as a humanitarian effort, it is unlikely that you are in a position to run your business and earn enough money to support you, your family and the operation—especially during the first year. Remember the old adage: It takes money to make money.

If you run a low-budget business you will probably get low-budget response. If you are determined to make it work, be sure you have sufficient capital to make it work the right way. Fear is often a factor: "I don't want to ask in case they say no." Well, that's the worst thing that can happen. But, if you persevere and are serious about your venture, someone will inevitably say yes!

And don't overlook friends and family; they can be your most ardent cheerleaders and supporters if you have given them reason in the past to believe you are responsible and determined to succeed.

B) *Know how much you need.* Lenders are familiar with the financial demands of business operation and will respect your request if you have obviously done your homework and can talk sensibly about your needs.

C) *Be direct and confident.* If you believe in your business and in your ability to make it work, others will be convinced. Never apologize for mistakes you feel you have made in the past and do not present the pathetic picture of someone who could make everything work if they just had enough money.
   Simply present the facts, even if they include revealing an error in judgment you have made somewhere along the line, and assure the lender that they will be making a smart decision by investing in you.

D) *Think positively.* If you need $50,000, ask for $50,000. Never underestimate the potential to provide. Even if you are approaching family members, you may be surprised to find that dear Cousin Fred has a $250,000 nest egg socked away. Anyway, it is easier to negotiate and deal with one lender for a single amount than it is to keep paperwork and relationships strong with several, all of whom have contributed a little to the pot.

E) *Ask again.* If they trusted you once and you have lived up to the stipulations of the contract, ask again and that goes for commercial lending institutions as well as friends and relatives. A proven record is what it's all about and if you have established yours, keep it active.

F) *Know when to borrow.* If you have worked out your business plan and know you can survive while getting the business off the ground, start exploring your financing options ahead of time. Don't wait until the last minute; this will force you to act frantically and could put you in the position of accepting a less than favorable situation. The same theory applies if your business is already established. By examining your financial position on a regular basis, you will be able to project how much you will need at a given point for expansion purposes. Be prepared.

G) *Don't borrow if it is not necessary.* Many businesses can be started for under $500. This is called "starting on a shoestring." Services, for example, often rely strictly on the owner's knowledge and expertise and can be set up quickly and inexpensively.

If this is the case with the business you have in mind, then try to avoid borrowing capital. It can be an expensive and timely proposition. In addition, if, after a projected period of time, the business is showing the kind of profit you can work with while growing, then the smart decision is to utilize the funds and put them back into the operation.

Establishing Credit

Is it possible to get a loan even if you have never established credit? Yes, it is. Many people in this country still prefer to pay cash, rather than incur high interest charges on loans or credit cards. They can still qualify for a loan based on personal assets or by having a friend or relative with a good credit rating who is willing to co-sign. This puts the obligation on the co-signer, so be sure the terms of the loan are clearly spelled out in a written agreement to the satisfaction of everyone involved in the transaction.

However, if your personal assets are minimal and you cannot find a co-signer, the best bet is to put off starting the business for four to six months while you establish credit. The best place to start is with a major department store such as Sears or J.C. Penney's.

They issue credit cards based on a very simple examination of your income and employment history. Charge about $100 worth of merchandise when you receive the card and pay it off according to the schedule provided. Within a few months, you will have proven yourself to be credit worthy, which will greatly improve your chances of getting a loan from a lending institution.

Another way to establish credit—and credibility—is to open a checking account at the bank you have decided to approach for a loan. They generally require a minimum deposit of between $50 and $100. Make it a point to meet the branch manager and/or the loan officer and to establish an ongoing relationship with them by stopping by to say hello when you are in the bank.

Within a few months, apply for a small personal loan, working with your new acquaintance, of course. Make your payments according to the prearranged schedule. Then when you are ready to request a more substantial amount of money to cover your start-up expenses, you will be recognized as a customer with a loan history at that institution.

14

RECORD-KEEPING: YOUR BUSINESS LIFELINE

The motivating factor in any business is profit, which can be explained as the money left over after all the bills, for everything from supplies to rent and salaries to taxes, are paid.

Building a profitable business is not something that can be left to chance; it must be planned and a systematic method of record-keeping must be developed to help you control income and expenses.

You should expect that during the early days of your business, your profits are going to be minimal as you become established. But it is possible, with even simple record-keeping procedures, to prepare yourself for lean periods and control day-to-day expenses to ensure that you are, at least, breaking even. In addition, financial records are required for tax purposes and dealing with them systematically can eliminate an incredibly overwhelming task at tax time.

Record-Keeping Can Be Simple

Some people cringe at the thought of record-keeping or feel it is a waste of valuable time. Usually, these attitudes are based on a lack of knowledge and the feeling that it is an overwhelming task. There is, however, no other way to analyze your cash flow and make sure you are pricing products or services high enough to realize a profit.

In actuality, record-keeping is not such a complicated process. If you have ever balanced a checkbook or planned a household budget, you have basically done several of the same steps necessary when implementing a bookkeeping system for your business. And the good news is that keeping your records does not have to be either complicated or time-consuming.

We know of entrepreneurs who opt for total simplicity by using the "shoebox" method—every sales record, receipt for expenses and bank statement gets tossed into a box. This system has two distinct drawbacks. One may not become apparent until tax time, when you attempt to wade through the paper to prepare your tax return. (If you hire an accountant to do your taxes, it shouldn't come as a surprise if an additional "combat fee" has been added to the bill.)

> *Goals are dreams with deadlines.*
>
> **Diana Scharf Hunt**

The other, more critical drawback is that it is virtually impossible to maintain an accurate picture of your financial situation when you stockpile, rather than record, business transactions. In order to understand your cash flow, it is important to be able to see what monies have come in, what you have paid out, current balances and outstanding debts.

In fact, you should be able to answer the following questions with just a quick review of your records:

- What was my income last year (week or month)?
- What were my expenses?
- How do income and expenses compare with last year (week or month)?
- What was my profit (or loss) last year (week or month)?
- Where can I cut back on expenses?
- Who and how much do I currently owe on outstanding debts?
- Who owes me money and how much?
- What are my assets, liabilities and net worth?
- Is my inventory in line with demand?
- How much cash do I have available? How much credit?
- Am I able to pay myself this month (week)?
- Are my figures in line with projected financial goals?

The primary documents that you need to be able to answer most of these questions are a Cash Journal, a Balance Sheet and a Bank Reconciliation. A simple single-entry system, as indicated on the following pages, in which to record disbursements (cash paid out) and receipts (cash taking in) forms the base of your record-keeping.

Double-Entry Bookkeeping

Your accountant will probably utilize a double-entry system, which involves recording each transaction twice: once as a debit (on the left column of the ledger) and once as a credit (the right column of the ledger). For example, if you were to sell a product for $100, the transactions recorded in a double-entry system would be as follows:

The $100 would be written as a credit in your Sales account, since merchandise is going out of the business and $100 would be recorded as a debit in your Cash account since money was coming into the business.

This is a complex and time-consuming process that is often best left to an accountant, as he or she will need the information to create a monthly Trial Balance and other financial statements, including your year-end tax reports.

Single-Entry Bookkeeping

You can, however, have your accountant's office set up a simple single-entry system for you which will tie in directly with their requirements. Or, check out the standardized bookkeeping systems, which provide all the necessary forms and documents in a bound book, stocked by stationery stores.

One of the most widely accepted, ready-made systems is the Dome Simplified Monthly Bookkeeping Record. It contains forms for recording monthly income and expenses, summary sheets from which you can create a Balance Sheet and listings of legal deductions for income tax reporting. Instructions are included.

In addition, the trade association for your field should be able to provide you with systems developed exclusively for use in the industry, which you can use "as-is" or adapt according to specific circumstances within your business.

The final method is to purchase a Cash Journal book and set up your own monthly system, as outlined below for Office Assistance, a small typing service, which has been operating for one month. Any of the above mentioned methods are acceptable, as long as you understand the entry process and can "read" the results.

Make Record-Keeping a Daily Task

The easiest way (short of paying someone else) to be sure your records are kept up-to-date is to incorporate the task into your daily or weekly routine. Many small business owners make it a habit to enter their sales, expenses and other financial information at the end of each working day. It keeps them continually aware of their financial situation and ensures that there will never be any unexpected cash-flow surprises. The process probably takes no more than 15 minutes for normal transactions, but will save hours of pencil-pushing and frustration down the line. And, more important, you'll know where you stand financially.

Setting Up the Books

Using Office Assistance, a secretarial service, as an example, we can examine the various elements required for basic record-keeping duties.

Bill Miller, president of Office Assistance, has been in business for one month. Two months ago, he opened a new business bank account with $10,000, his start-up capital from a personal savings account.

At the same time, he rented a small office in a downtown building for $350.00 a month, but had to pay first month rent and a deposit of the last month's rent, for a total outlay of $700.

His fictitious name statement, which he got approved

Debit & Credit in Bookkeeping

Debits include
- Cash receipts
- Purchases
- Expenses, such as rent and wages

Credits include:
- Cash payments
- Sales of services or merchandise.
- Earnings, including interest earned

through the local county clerk's office, ran $10.00 and publishing it in a regional newspaper cost $45.00.

The initial month's lease and a deposit on a state-of-the-art typewriter cost him $275.00, plus $50.00 for a maintenance agreement. However, he will own the $2,000 typewriter when his payment schedule is completed.

He found a brand new calculator at a garage sale for $25.00 and is going to use a desk, table, lamp and chairs brought from home (value $350.00) to decorate the office. Phone installation was $150.00, but he purchased a two-line telephone for $79.50.

An artist friend designed his logo and letterhead on a computer for only $25 and a $6.95 lunch. He had his stationery ($35.00), business cards ($60.00) and brochures ($23.50) produced through a local copy shop for a total of $118.50.

A 2 x 2 inch display ad in the local newspaper cost him $370.00 for a week, and he is planning to mail 100 of his brochures to local businesses selected from the phone book. Stamps: $25.00 for the mailing. Office supplies, including typing paper, staples, paper clips, etc., set him back $45.00. A journal for record-keeping cost $7.95.

He purchased a packet of invoices for $5.95 and, during the first month, has billed and been paid $700.00. However, he has two accounts who still owe him a total of $400. Bill dutifully records information in his cash journal at the end of each working day. He uses source documents, including his checkbook register, receipts from cash purchases and billing invoices as the basis for his entries. The two pages following are for May (prior to opening the doors of his business) and June (his first actual month in business).

Office Assistance
Cash Journal for May

Date	Check # Invoice #	Detail	(Debit) Expense	(Credit) Income
5/1	100	Rawlins Real Estate (Rent & dep)	$700.00	
5/5	101	County Clerk (Fictitious Name)	10.00	
5/7	102	The Herald (publishing FNS)	45.00	
5/9	103	Ed's Keyboards (IBM 1-mo. & dep)	275.00	
5/9	104	Ed's Keyboards (Maint. agreement)	50.00	
5/12	105	Mary Smith (Calculator purchase)	25.00	
5/18	106	Telephone company (line installation)	150.00	
5/20	107	Phone Store (2-line phone)	79.50	
5/22	108	Ray Brown (logo design)	25.00	
5/24	Cash	The Hungry Dog (lunch/Ray Brown)	6.95	
5/28	109	The Copy Spot (brochures, cards, etc.)	35.00	
5/29	110	The Herald (advertising)	370.00	
		Total Income & Expense (May)	**$1,771.45**	**$0.00**

Office Assistance
Cash Journal for June

Date	Check # Invoice #	Detail	(Debit) Expense	(Credit) Income
6/4	111	U.S.P.O (Stamps for mailing)	$ 25.00	
6/6	112	Office Stationers (supplies, invoices, etc.)	58.90	
6/7	A1	W. Smith		$ 62.50
6/8	A2	Art Association		112.50
6/9	A3	T. Williams		22.00
6/9	113	Judy Miller (typing fee)	100.00	
6/10	A4	Bank of Cutterville		75.00
6/10	A5	WKTR-FM		120.50
6/13	A6	J. Johnson		43.50
6/15	114	Rawlins Real Estate (rent)	350.00	
6/15	A7	C. Lewis		73.50
6/15	A8	R. Swell		90.00
6/16	115	Judy Miller (typing fee)	100.00	
6/19	A9	W. Smith		52.50
6/23	116	Judy Miller (typing fee)	100.00	
6/26	117	Phone company (bill)	15.90	
6/27	A10	K. Black		48.00
6/30	118	Judy Miller (typing fee)	100.00	

Total Income & Expense (June) $765.90 $700.00

Bill's expenses for May and June were $2,537.35. Of course, part of that is for start-up expenses, such as deposits on his rent and typewriter, installation costs and one-time fictitious name filing and publishing. His income for the first month was $700. By deducting his expenses from his income, he can see that, at the moment, his business is showing a loss of $1,837.35.

Although Bill has been in business for only a month, he is curious about his company's financial worth and decides to work up a balance sheet to get the answer. The calculation, as indicated in the following example, is the amount owned (assets) minus the amount due to creditors (liabilities) which equals his worth.

Balance Sheet as of June 30

Assets		Liabilities	
Cash on hand & in bank	$ 8,162.54	Ed's Keyboards	$ 1,725.00
(Capital balance & June Income)		*(Balance on IBM)*	
Office Equipment	2,104.50	Unpaid rent *(July)*	350.00
(includes full value of IBM		Taxes *(estimated)*	75.00
even though not paid off)			
Office Furniture	350.00		
Accounts Receivable		**Liabilities**	$ 2,150.00
(outstanding invoices			
for work already done)	400.00		
Total Assets	$11,017.04	*CAPITAL	$ 8,867.04
		Total Liabilities	$11,017.04

The figure Bill is most interested in is the *CAPITAL amount in the Liabilities column. This is the amount remaining after what Bill owes is subtracted from his current assets and is what his business is worth at the end of

June. In other words, if he decided to try to sell his business right now, he could realistically ask that amount as a sales price. Of course, Bill probably wouldn't get that amount because he has not yet become established enough to warrant someone buying the business, unless they were looking for a "turnkey" operation—in other words, a business they could just walk into and get going immediately.

This information is valuable when Bill goes to apply for expansion capital or for credit on future purchases he plans to make, i.e., a photocopier, a computer and new furniture. His balance sheet will change each time he prepares it (probably quarterly in the future) as business increases bringing in more income and reducing his debts.

In the meantime, the Balance Sheet gives Bill a tool to use when comparing the financial standing of his business this month against future months and years. It also keeps him current on what he owns, whom he owes money to and his major sources of income.

The same procedure is used in developing a personal balance sheet, which possibly would be needed to establish credibility when applying for a loan. Assets would include furniture, automobiles, jewelry, your home and other tangibles, while liabilities would consist of outstanding loans and other major debts.

Bank Statement Reconciliation

Another important step that Bill must handle monthly is reconciling his bank statement against his checkbook register. He simply marks off the checks in his register that have cleared per the statement and the deposits which have been credited, and deducts any service charges for the previous month from his balance.

Bill then adds up all the outstanding checks—those listed in his register which have not cleared by the closing date indicated on the bank statement—and deducts them from the balance indicated on his bank statement. He adds up any deposits which have not yet been credited to his account and then *adds* them to the balance, as indicated below.

Balance per bank statement	$ 7,953.44
Plus: Deposits not credited	+ 325.00
Minus: Outstanding checks	- 115.90
New Balance	$ 8,162.54

The new balance figure should match that listed in his checkbook register and, in this case, it does. If, however, the statement and the register did not reconcile, Bill would have a customer representative at the bank review his statement and banking activity for the past month.

Pricing in General

One of the toughest problems that small business owners face is establishing prices that, on one hand, the market will bear while, on the other, will cover overhead and guarantee a profit.

Often new business owners give the business away to get sales, but this is not an advisable practice. Realistic pricing indicates your confidence in what you are selling, and if you value your service, so will the customer.

Today's consumer realizes that they can't get something worthwhile for nothing, so don't be afraid to establish prices that will work toward your profit goals.

Pricing Guidelines

Several factors must be taken into consideration when setting prices:

a) **The cost of goods sold.** In the case of a retail or wholesale operation, this is the amount originally paid for the goods, while for a manufacturer, it involves the cost of producing the goods. In the case of a service business, overhead expenses and equipment costs must be taken into account.

b) **The nature of the product or service.** Uniqueness and demand come into play here. In the case of goods with a stable level of demand, such as bread or auto repair, the raising or lowering of prices will have little effect. However, when demand is high for goods that are hard to get, the price can realistically be set anywhere the owner wants.

c) **The competition.** Recognize what your competition is charging, for often this will guide pricing within a certain region. However, if a competitor is charging what you feel is an unrealistic price—either more or less—for a product or service, you owe it to yourself to find out why. Then set your prices according to all of the factors outlined here.

Even if they are higher than the competitor's, consumers will pay the price if you can offer an advantage, such as a friendly atmosphere, convenient hours or some other benefit not provided by the competition.

d) **Company policy.** This encompasses a number of things, including your location, your position in the marketplace, the additional services offered and takes into account your personal philosophy about business and your role in it.

e) **Market strategy.** Should you go for large volume at low prices or for low volume at high prices? That is the bottom line in considering market strategy. As a small business owner, you will likely opt for low volume and higher prices since the alternative involves having the resources, including labor, display room, distribution channels, etc., to move large volumes of product or perform major service tasks.

f) **Customers.** What will the market bear? In other words, what are your customers willing to pay for your products or services?

People expect prices that are fair; if you are planning to charge overinflated rates you had better be a top-notch salesperson or offer something so unusual that the price won't matter.

Although there are differences between establishing prices for retail operations, wholesale products, manufacturing and services, the basic formula for price setting is:

Labor + Materials + Overhead + Profit Margin = Selling Price

However, before setting prices on goods or services, it is extremely important to understand the concept of the Break-Even Point. Many small business owners operate on an overall profit-loss basis without realizing the importance of cost accounting. Being aware of such factors as your break-even point, markup and profit margin can tell you which areas of your business are profitable and which are causing a drain.

Understanding Break-Even

The break-even point is the minimum amount you must charge in order to cover all expenses incurred for the production and promotion of your goods and/or services without losing or making money. In other words, any income which is above the break-even point is considered to be profit and anything below it is a loss.

To find your break-even point, you must first total all of your operating costs, including materials and labor, equipment lease or purchase payments, advertising, utilities, office supplies and any incidentals such as gasoline, maintenance, postage, etc.

Generally, this is computed for a particular period of time, such as six months or a year. However, if your business is still in the early stages of operation, you can use the estimated figures on your projected expenses statement (outlined Section III) and "guesstimate" costs for materials and labor.

For example, the monthly expenses for a hypothetical cake-decorating business total $300 a month. You want to know what the break-even point would be if you sell an average of 20 cakes per month. The calculation is as follows:

$$\$300 \text{ (expenses)} \div 20 \text{ cakes} = \$15.00$$

In order to break even, that is, without losing money or realizing a profit, you must charge a minimum of $15 for each cake sold.

The same process can be used to analyze the break-even point on a weekly basis. First you determine your annual expenses by multiplying the $300 by 12 months, which would give you $3,600 per year.

The calculation to find the weekly break-even point is:

$3,600 (expenses) ÷ 52 weeks = $69.23

Therefore, you must earn $69.23 per week to operate the business without losing money and without realizing a profit.

Stay Informed

Knowing your break-even point is one of the greatest favors you can do for yourself as a business owner. It tells you how much you must charge for your products or services and serves as an invaluable tool in setting prices which will help you realize a profit.

Keep in mind, however, that the break-even point is a variable figure. Since it depends on production and overhead costs, plan to reevaluate periodically to make sure your prices reflect any changes.

Labor Costs

Labor costs, obviously, are the expenses incurred for the actual work done to manufacture or sell a product or to perform a service. Think of them as wages or salaries. Small business owners often end up working for free because they fail to set a wage for themselves. Despite the fact that you want to reinvest all of the income received back into the business for awhile, it is imperative that you establish a fixed salary amount for yourself when figuring operating expenses.

If you have set aside a survival fund to carry you through the first six months or so of operation, you may want to defer your salary until the business becomes solvent; however, you should still figure the amount into your expenses. Otherwise, you may find the prices you set are too low to justify making a profit from the onset.

It is much easier to set realistic prices from the beginning than it is to raise them later in an attempt to make up the difference. Remember, your time and skills are the cornerstone of your business, so think of paying yourself as you would any valuable employee.

Setting Retail Prices

If you are manufacturing items to sell at retail prices, without using a middleman, the following formula is a good basis to start with when establishing a selling price for your inventory of goods.

1/3 Labor + 1/3 Materials & Overhead + 1/3 Profit = Selling Price

---

You need a starting point. One place to start is with your labor costs. If, for example, the monetary value of your time and effort (labor) in producing an item is $6, you allocate $6 for material and overhead and an additional $6 as profit for a total selling price of $18.

If materials and overhead are costing more, you can: a) boost the price accordingly, b) review your expenses and find ways to cut back on material costs, such as finding a less expensive supplier or c) utilize a portion of the profit margin to cover the balance. Of the three options, b) is the best way to go.

You must also remember that when you are producing mass quantities of an item, your costs will be reduced because of price breaks on supplies and reduced labor costs per unit. You're then able to structure your selling price according to previously mentioned pricing factors, such as competition and demand for the product.

If you are starting a retail business that relies on selling products you purchase at wholesale, you may have some of your prices set for you by what the competition is doing or recommendations made by the wholesaler. However, there will still be items which you must price yourself.

This will involve understanding the principle of markup or gross margin—the difference between the cost of goods sold and the selling price, taking into consideration sale markdowns, shortages and discounts to employees. Generally, markup is stated as a percentage of retail price.

For example, if a manufacturer sells dresses to you at a wholesale price of $12.50 each and you sell them for $25, you would have a 100% markup (a 50% gross margin).

If you know the cost of goods and the average amount of markup you need to operate profitably, it is relatively simple to determine a price by using the following formula:

$$\frac{\text{Cost of goods}}{100 - \text{markup} \%} \times 100 = \text{Retail Price}$$

For example, if you purchased a gross of rubber ducks for a total price of $172.80 and had determined that you needed a gross margin of 36% to operate profitably, you would calculate the expected profit as follows, using the equation above:

$$\frac{\$172.80}{100 - 36} \times 100 = \$270.00$$

When you divide the Retail Price ($270.00) by the number of items (144: a gross) you get a unit price of $1.88, which you would probably raise to $1.98, depending on the market, to improve the profit margin slightly and provide leeway for markdowns during sales, etc.

Specialty items, such as antiques, artwork, imported goods and handcrafted items can be priced higher according to current value and what the market in your area will bear. They generally run between a 200% and 300% markup range.

Setting Wholesale Prices

Operating as a wholesale manufacturer greatly reduces your selling and administrative costs, because you are passing your products on to someone else to sell. Your price to retailers should thus be approximately 50% less than the suggested retail price.

In actuality, you are providing retailers with a discount because of their willingness and ability to promote your product.

The formula for wholesale pricing includes your profit margin + labor costs + expenses, which will be appreciably lower than for a retail operation because of savings on advertising, display equipment and maintenance, but which must include warehousing and marketing.

Money is a sixth sense which makes it possible for us to enjoy the other five senses.

Richard Ney

Pricing is typically more competitive at the wholesale level than at any other and is almost always the determining factor in whether your products are purchased or not.

Also affecting wholesalers are other wholesalers offering competitive pricing, middlemen buying large quantities at low prices and supply and demand factors.

As a wholesaler, you are in a position to vary prices according to the size of orders and your ability to negotiate with buyers. However, it is a good idea to develop a solid markup base from which to operate. This will allow you the flexibility to offer maximum and minimum prices for each item based on quantity buys.

Pricing is a crucial aspect of managing your business. Since you are in business to make a profit, it is important that you set prices which will result in the greatest income.

To do this, you must know what your costs are, or at least, have a solid idea of projected costs if you are still in the process of planning your venture.

By not setting prices that are too high or too low for the product or service you are selling, you will be assured of a favorable position in the market and a healthy share of the wealth.

Setting Prices for Home Inspection

Rates for home inspection vary according to area. People in Malibu, California, considering the purchase of a $1.2 million "beach house" will be willing to spend more money for an inspection than someone in rural Kansas. They will also usually have more to inspect like high-tech alarm systems, pools and guest houses.

Some sources say that an inspector's services are worth one dollar per thousand of the home's value. In other words, a $200,000 home would bring a $200 inspection fee. While this is a good rule of thumb in well-to-do metropolitan areas where house values are high, it does not work as well in less substantial areas of the country.

Age of the home must also be a consideration. If you have to inspect the wiring and plumbing on a 200-year-old New England farm house, and poke in and out of odd-sized crawl spaces, it will take longer.

Many inspectors work strictly on an hourly basis. This is a good system in that you can easily estimate what your weekly, monthly and yearly earnings will be based on the amount of hours you are booking. The disadvantage to this system is that owners or bankers may try to rush you through your inspection to save money. Once you have a few inspections under your belt, though, you will be able to estimate how long an inspection will take and pass this estimate along to the client. Your hourly rate must be high enough to be considered a successful business—pay all the bills and support your family (or at least half of it in a two-income family).

The best way to determine what you should charge is to find out what other home inspectors are charging. If you had an inspection done on your home, use that as a guideline. If you know someone who had an inspection done recently, ask them. Finally, you can call around and get estimates from inspectors listed in the area phone book. Ask about several different house sizes and styles to get a range of prices. $25-$50 per hour to start seems to be acceptable to most clients. Always try to include a minimum number of hours. As we indicated in the Introduction, a thorough inspection can take three to five hours. As your experience and your reputation grow you can increase your rates. Try not to be the most expensive home inspector in your area or the cheapest. People tend to think they are not getting full service if the price is too cheap. Conversely, they think they are getting ripped off if the price is too high.

> *Although there are countless alumni of the school of hard knocks, there has not yet been a move to accredit that institution.*
>
> *Sonya Rudikoff*

If after all your research you still have not come up with an hourly rate consider this: you are now self-employed. You have to cover your own health insurance, retirement insurance, paid vacations. You must pay all the regular taxes plus self-employment taxes. You may need to hire a bookkeeper or a tax consultant. Plus, you need to consider the other overhead costs associated with running a business. Your expenses have just gone up 30%-50%. You need to recoup that. Also, unless you are different than most people, you are probably making less than you need to live on at your present job (which is one of the reasons to become a home inspector). Finally, you have to consider that you will have many weeks when you work less than forty hours a week.

When you take this all into consideration you will see that you probably need to at least double your present hourly rate of pay, maybe triple it.

Inventory as Investment

Ask 100 small business owners what inventory means to them and more than 90% will tell you it's the merchandise they keep on hand to sell to their customers or the materials and supplies stocked to produce goods or perform a service.

This is partially accurate, for inventory can and should be viewed as any supplies, raw materials or finished goods used to generate a profit in your business. But it isn't the response that a savvy business owner would give.

Surprisingly, according to a recent study conducted by a leading consulting firm, less than 10% of a group of 500 entrepreneurs interviewed spoke of their inventory in terms of the investment it represents; an investment that can range from 15% to 25% percent of total operating capital.

It is because of this "misunderstanding" that many small business owners often fail to incorporate good inventory control practices into their regular management routine. Although they keep an eagle eye on every penny going through the books, they may totally overlook the cash tied up in their inventory.

Controlling Inventory

Inventory control can be a very simple, straightforward task if you implement a workable system from the beginning — preferably even before you start ordering and receiving goods. You will find that time really flies when you are self-employed and it's easy to postpone such tasks as inventory control until, one day, you find yourself facing an overwhelming job.

Inventory control will give you valuable information about: a) Whether or not you are carrying too much or too little inventory based on, for example, items and prices preferred by your customers, or seasonal aspects, and b) whether you are realizing optimum economy determined by the costs of storage, taxes, handling and the investment per unit.

The ideal situation is to maintain an inventory that is profitable because it turns over (comes in and goes out of the business) regularly, lowering the cost of storing, displaying and insuring it.

There are several methods of inventory control that you can adopt, depending on your business. The main goal with each method, however, is to tell you how many items you have on hand and how many you need to meet your customer or production demands. It will also work toward lessening inventory shrinkage, which is generally the result of employee pilferage, customer theft, storing inventory incorrectly or maintaining sloppy records of items ordered, received and used.

You can tell how many items you currently have by making an educated guess, which generally only works for businesses having a small, visible inventory that is relatively predictable. An example of the kind of business which could probably operate efficiently with this "relaxed" form of inventory control would be a one- or two-person enterprise that monthly goes through, say, a box of invoices and similar supplies available for a minimum amount at the discount office-supply store.

Other methods of inventory control are the physical count, which should be done at least once a year anyway for tax purposes, or—the easiest and most efficient of them all—maintaining an ongoing record. The best idea is to incorporate the latter two systems; by backing up periodic physical counts with a perpetual record.

To set up your perpetual system, simply create a file card or inventory sheet set up in a three-ring binder for each item in your inventory. Across the top of the card or sheet, list the following:

a) item name and a code number, if applicable
b) a description of the item,
c) where it is stored,
d) the supplier's name, address & phone number,
e) unit price (i.e., $12.95/dozen),
f) your selling price (if a retail item) or percentage of gross price of completed product (if used for manufacturing) or service,
g) the date you place an order, and
h) the number of items and the date they are received.

Then, every time you sell or use an item, write it down and subtract it from the last balance. You should also indicate reorder number, based on when and by how much you must replenish your stock. The reorder number will be determined by such factors as: a) the minimum cost per unit available from your supplier, including quantity discounts, preseason specials and discounts for cash or quick payment, b) the delivery schedule, from the time you place the order until you receive it, and c) economic and social trends which can affect the way an item is perceived by the public.

For example, during a period of depressed or inflated economy, sales for leisure items typically drop. By keeping an eye on these factors, you can adjust your inventory needs accordingly and not get stuck with great quantities of items that you can't move.

After a while, you will be able to recognize at a glance which items are regularly used and which are simply taking up shelf space. When you reach this point, your ordering skills will become much more efficient and your investment in inventory will become a profitable proposition.

15

ORGANIZATION:
TIME-MANAGEMENT TIPS

A recent survey of small business owners indicated that one of the qualities they felt contributed the most to their success was organization. In conjunction with this is the fact that time management and basic organizational seminars continue to be the most popular offerings in adult education catalogs and business workshops around the country.

Time is money! Because the small business owner is plagued by a unique set of problems, such as continual interruptions and overworking, it is vital to your success that you learn to manage your time and organize paperwork. This might sound rather simplistic, but you would be amazed at the number of small business owners who operate in a constant state of chaos.

Although we have seen a number of "A messy office is the sign of a creative mind" posters on entrepreneur's office walls, it is a good bet that the holders of these signs can recount story after story of missing checks, lost orders and misplaced files that totally disrupted the flow of business until they were located in a corner pile.

The survey respondents also stated that once they had learned to manage their time in both their personal and business lives and had set up guidelines for handling routine tasks, they felt more confident about accepting new challenges and making decisions.

The simple truth about getting organized is that it clears your mind for taking care of the nitty-gritty, profit-making aspects of being in business—production and promotion. For example, by allotting a certain place in your desk to hold customer files and billing information, you have made one major step towards maximizing production. Knowing that all the needed supplies and materials are located in one spot saves you valuable time and energy.

Making Time Work for You

Time management is the ability to take the hours we have available and use them to our advantage. Making lists of tasks to be done and giving them a priority rating is one of the best ways to avoid losing precious moments.

Keep a monthly calendar handy to help you keep track of major commitments, important dates and appointments. Try to avoid using it for notations of daily work in progress, carry-over tasks or other things that are best suited for inclusion on your daily and weekly lists.

There are several other ideas you can easily incorporate into your working lifestyle that will maximize your productivity.

• *Work smart.* Handle the jobs you find most difficult or cumbersome during peak performance time. If you are a morning person and find that making telephone calls to potential customers is one of your least favorite responsibilities, take care of them first thing in the morning when you are feeling fresh and energetic, and organize the rest of the day's tasks accordingly.

• *Set realistic daily goals for yourself.* Just because you are chief cook and bottlewasher, don't try to do everything at once. Learn just how much work you can accept and expect to accomplish in a given period of time and allow yourself to turn down work if it seems like it will be too much for you to handle.

• *Reward yourself.* When you are working alone, as many small business owners do when getting their businesses off the ground, there generally aren't many people anywhere around to support or praise your work . . . and everyone needs strokes! While it is true that a customer's praises are an indication that you are doing the right thing, you still need time to relax.

Treat yourself to a special dinner once a week. If money is especially tight, plan an evening where you go to bed early with a good book or do something that has absolutely nothing to do with business. And remind yourself that this is your reward for accomplishing certain goals for the week. It will help to keep your spirits high.

• *Don't procrastinate.* Don't put off doing tasks that must be done. If you constantly let some tasks slide because you don't enjoy doing them, you will soon find yourself terribly backlogged and unable to catch up. The effects of this may not show themselves until you are faced with a deadline and, at that point, you will discover that you are working at less than maximum efficiency, feeling tense and being hassled by small things. Even when business is slow and it seems that there could be little harm done by taking a day off to visit with a friend, be sure to complete required tasks before closing up shop.

• *Limit personal phone calls* during established business hours. Personal calls not only eat into productive time, they tie up the line when an important client may be trying to get in touch with you. The same holds true with friendly visitations. If you are self-employed, friends often feel that you are not really 'working' and can stop anytime to chat. Explain that you will be happy to visit with them at a specific time and be sure to tell them why, so there aren't any ruffled feathers.

Obviously, there will be times when unavoidable situations, such as an emergency or an unexpected problem, arise. Try to take these inevitabilities into consideration by estimating how long a project will take and then adding a bit of extra time to give yourself leeway.

• *Delegate.* If you find that you absolutely cannot handle a certain aspect of the business, such as your own bookkeeping, for example, don't labor over the task—you will end up wasting a great deal of time and could make some serious mistakes. Admit to yourself that the task is just not a strong point and have someone else do it.

• *Learn to say no.* One of the hardest things for most people to do is to say "no." Even when we realize that, for example, helping a friend out on a special project will eat into valuable time, we often agree to do such things because we hate to say no. What we do is justify our acceptance by assuring ourselves that saying yes will put us in the position of meeting a lot of potential customers. The reality is that using that time to make phone calls or a sales call for your own business will probably result in a paying customer, not just a potential contact.

• *Minimize business meetings.* Before setting up a formal meeting, which can be very time-consuming, see if you can take care of the matter in question by phone or through the mail. If a meeting can't be avoided, make sure you specify a time limit to encourage people to get down to business. Another time-saving device for meetings is to work up an agenda that outlines exactly what has to be discussed to avoid idle chit-chat and unnecessary diversions.

• *Plan your time.* When you have to run errands, plan them for a time that is most convenient, such as in the morning when traffic is light. Plan to do as many things as possible in one trip, outlining the stops you must make so they follow a sequential order.

16

HOME INSPECTION OPERATIONS

Let's start at the beginning—the checklist. Although you will probably refine and revise your checklist as you gain experience, we have given you one to start with that we think covers most things. As we mentioned earlier, many inspectors include diagrams of things like water heaters, heating plants and roofing, so that they can pinpoint problem areas. We have included a few, others can be found in specialty books in the local library, which you can make copies of as needed.

Ron Martin likes to do a quick visual of the outside, then head right to the attic, work his way to the basement and then do a comprehensive landscape check and roof check at the end of his inspection. Other inspectors like to start with the landscaping. There is a good reason for this. If a house has negative pitch, meaning water runoff will run back into the house instead of away from the house, then that constitutes a major problem—especially in wet climates or climates that get large rainfalls all in a short season—like California.

We have set up our checklist to start outside then move inside and go top to bottom. Because some heating systems will be found in the attic while others will be found in the basement, we have included both heating systems and hot water heaters as separate sections.

Note also that we have set up the checklist with extra space at the top right. Until you design your own, you can copy this one and use that space to add your company name and phone number. One way to do this is to have an inexpensive rubber stamp made. You can also just write your name and number in or type it in on a typewriter. Your checklist can stand alone as the final report, although we suggest a cover letter accompany the report. The cover letter allows you to mention any specifics and thank the clients for choosing your firm. While, it may be years before they require your services again, they may pass your name along to others.

Let's go through the checklist, section by section.

External

Check the grading. You are checking for negative pitch in the grading or with the slab. Use your marble on hard surfaces. If it rolls toward the house, so will water. You'll also need to check for holes, cracks and unevenness in the foundation, driveways, walkways, and patio and pool areas. Severe lifting on any of these surfaces may be caused by tree roots. Point out the suspect tree on your report.

Check the landscaping. The condition of front and back yards often indicates how the home was cared for. Any signs of standing water on the property may indicate poor drainage. Are plantings in good shape? If grass needs replanting are there at least 5 inches of topsoil? Is lawn in good shape? Putting in a new lawn can be very expensive. Do any trees appear diseased or infested? Are they pruned? Are any trees too close to the house with heavy branches resting on dormers or roof edges?

If there are fences, check for dry rot with your screwdriver. Walls should be checked for loose stones or bricks. If there is a retaining wall, does it appear upright and solid or will it need reinforcing?

Sometimes a house will settle differently from the porch or steps. This can lead to separation. Check the porch for sagging. Also, if a porch is made from wood and the support posts are in direct contact with the ground, there may be dry rot and termites.

At this point it should be noted that many lenders today require a complete termite inspection. If you find any evidence, like small channels in dry rot or small pellets or sawdust (this may indicate carpenter ants), recommend a complete termite/insect inspection by a professional. Also suggest that they have any support posts redone with cement footings to prevent further infestations.

From the grounds you can get a good look at the roof line and chimney (use your binoculars). In climates with heavy snowfall the roof line can start to sag. This is not good. Also, chimneys should not lean at all and should not be missing bricks. If you actually climb onto the roof, check for a spark arrestor and a weather protective hood over the chimney. Tap the chimney lightly with your hammer. If there are any loose bricks, suggest an expert be called.

Check gutters and downspouts. Downspouts should transport water several feet away from the house. Look for evidence of staining on the outside of the home. This could indicate that the gutters are clogged or broken. Also check the flashing. Flashing prevents water from running back up under the shakes (or whatever) and roofing paper. If you find water damage inside the attic, this could be the problem.

Check the finish of the house. If it is paint, is it peeling, chipping or flaking? If brick, check the mortar. Is there chronic cracking? Are there holes in stucco walls? Do windows need caulking? If there is an attached garage, does it appear original or is it an add-on? If you note any add-ons, make sure they are approved. Many people have construction done without permits. The city or county can make the new owner tear down and remove any unapproved structural work. If you suspect add-ons, inform the client to make sure the plans were approved.

You should also make sure outdoor lighting is working properly and appears up to code.

Internal

Let's do like Ron Martin does and start at the top—the attic. Some attics are finished, so they have walls, floors and ceilings covering the insulation. Still, there should be a crawl space in one corner where you can see or not see any insulation. If you have access, measure the depth of the insulation. On older homes you may run into asbestos. If you think there may be asbestos, wear a mask—and inform the client.

All attics are vented. They help the house breathe. Vents can be clogged with branches, leaves or nesting animals. If louvered vents, make sure the louvers are working.

Check for dampness or staining from old leaks. Some homes leak only when it rains really hard. If you suspect a leak, or if you want to check to make sure gutters are clear, you can place a hose on the roof for ten or fifteen minutes and check your results.

Check the chimney where it runs through the attic for cracks or other signs of damage, also check any vents like from bathrooms.

Moving into the bedrooms, check the walls and ceilings for cracking, chipping and peeling paint or wallpaper. Also eyeball for squareness. You can also use your carpenter's square to check. Look at the floor. If it is hardwood, what shape is it in. Does it need to be refinished? Are there any dings and gouges or stains? As you walk do the floorboards squeak? This means that flooring, subflooring or framing is loose. This can be expensive. Most hardwood floors are tongue and groove. If the floor has been sanded and refinished too many times, the tongue and groove may be too close to the surface. This means that it cannot be refinished and will have to be replaced or covered with carpeting.

Check windows for ease of operation, tightness and type. Double pane glass is much better than single pane. If there is an air conditioning unit in the window, make sure it is working and properly sealed against leaks.

Use your electrical tester to check all the outlets. Make note of any that are not working. Also check the tightness of the receptacles by plugging in a plug. It should not wiggle around or hang loose.

Check privacy door and closet doors for ease of operation and tightness when closed. Make sure locks are working.

In the rest of the rooms you will follow most of the same rules as in the bedrooms, checking the walls, floors, ceilings, outlets, etc. Check carpeting in all rooms. It should not be loose (try grabbing it with your fingers and see if you can pull it up). It should not be pulling away from the walls. This indicates shrinkage or poor installation. You should not be able to see the seams where carpet has been pieced together. Also check for fading, wearing and discolorations, especially in high-traffic areas.

Moving into the kitchen, you will need to check the counters and cabinets for chipping, cracking, etc. Also look inside cabinets for sign of infestation and dampness.

Check the outlets with your tester. Check the garbage disposal. Check the trash compactor. And then you will want to check all the major appliances. Turn things on. Smell them. Listen to them. Run the dishwasher for a complete cycle. Start up the stove. If it is gas, does it smell okay or is there a lingering gas odor that could indicate leaking? Try the oven to see if it heats quickly and smells okay.

Turn on the faucet, then quickly turn it off. If the pipes bang and pound then you have a water hammer, caused by a combination of loose pipes and lack of air stops. Adding air stops can fix this problem but may run several hundred dollars. Make sure you note this. Run the water hard for several minutes then check for leaks under the sink. Check water pressure with your gauge. You should do this with all sinks.

In the bathrooms, in addition to the things we have already discussed, you will want to check the tub and shower for cracking or chipping, also of course for any staining or leaking.

Check the toilet for leaks and efficiency of operation. One way you can check for blockage is to drop a significant amount of toilet tissue into the bowl and flush. The water should go down. If it rises first then goes down there is some blockage and that should be noted. If the bathroom is tiled, make sure it is ceramic tile and not plastic. Plastic tile comes in small squares, which cannot be grouted so it cannot be sealed against leaks. Many internal bathrooms now have skylights. Skylights can be in other rooms as well. Check for tightness against leaks. Again, a hose placed on the roof around the skylight will reveal if the contractor set up a good water path around the skylight and whether it leaks. Skylights that open should have sealing gaskets checked. Also in the bathroom, make sure exhaust fans are working properly. You should have seen the exhaust vent in the attic and exiting on the roof. Make sure it is clear.

Garages serve many purposes. Make sure that garage door openers work properly and that outlets are working. Remember that garage wall outlets, outdoor receptacles and bathroom outlets should have a GFCI protecting the circuit. Make note if these are not present. Also check the insulation in garages, especially those walls that connect to the house.

The biggest problems with water heaters are leaking or blockage. Leaking is caused by rusted fittings and tanks. Blockage can occur in areas with hard water. Mineral deposits build up, narrowing capacity and lowering efficiency. Look for a date of installation. Any water heater over ten years old should be replaced. Make sure the water heater is properly strapped to the wall. Also look for flexible copper connections. These will be less likely to snap during an earthquake, or some other natural disaster. Gas water heaters should be checked for gas leaks with your gas leak detector.

Heating systems can make or break the sale of a home. To replace a heating system can cost thousands of dollars. There are many types of heaters. In warm climates, small electric or gas furnaces that force hot air through the house are all that is required. In colder climates heating with hot water or steam is more popular.

Water heaters require a boiler, an expansion tank atop the boiler, a safety valve, a thermometer and a circulating pump. The circulating pump is the most suspect part of the system, as it is prone to leaks. Also you will want to check the mechanical gauges to make sure they are functioning properly and heating the water to 180 degrees. The other thing to check, of course, is the pipes. They should be copper and should be full of water all the time. Hot water radiators should have a working bleed valve on them so that air can be let out of the pipes to avoid a sloshing sound during operation.

A steam boiler heats water to 212 degrees where it turns to steam. The steam boiler must always have water in it. There should be a glass viewing window (sight glass) on the outside so you can observe the level. There are safety features (ball cock) that won't allow the boiler to operate if there is no water. On top of this ball cock is a bleeder valve. With the boiler running, hit the bleeder valve. When the ball cock drops to below horizontal, the boiler should shut off. Steam radiators have shut-off valves. If the valve sticks it will let steam out into the room in the form of a spray, which lowers heat, or not let steam into the radiator at all, which eliminates heat. Bad valves cannot be fixed. They must be replaced.

Central air heating systems rely on gravity or forced air. Gravity systems are big units and use very large duct work. Naturally, they are usually in the basement as they work on the principle that hot air rises. Forced air units use a fan to drive the heat. On both units a heat exchanger adds heat to the air before it is circulated. This unit is in a firebox. The firebox should never be too hot to the touch. If it is, it needs service immediately.

These units almost always need a new thermocoupler. The thermocoupler is a safety device that shuts down the unit if the pilot light goes out. They are inexpensive to replace and that should be suggested. On forced air units fan belts should be checked for wear and filters should be checked and usually replaced. Also with hot air, a humidifier is preferential because hot air dries out a house. If the unit has one, check for rusting and leaking. If it doesn't have one, alert the client. Finally, both units have air-flow controls that allow you to adjust the heat to different registers so that one room doesn't get too hot and another too cold. Make sure these dampers are working.

There are a few more things to check in older homes that may be important to the new owners. Most older homes have 100 amps of power. This is probably sufficient power for a six-room house with normal appliances. Most newer homes have been designed with 200 amps of power to meet the needs of more and more high-energy appliances. Amps should be marked on the fuse/circuit breaker box. You may find an older house with only 60 amp service. This is almost an automatic update and you should suggest that the client contact an electrician for a cost estimate.

A 100 amp house may be broken down to six 15 amp circuits or two 20 amp and four 15 amp circuits. A kitchen and laundry room will both require a 20 amp circuit. The kitchen will also require up to two 15 amp circuits. This is okay because normal bedroom use is light and one 15 amp circuit can handle two bedrooms. But if the client is going to have more than the normal amount of appliances, they may not be satisfied with a 100 amp home.

You should also make sure the house has copper wiring. For a short period, aluminum wiring was popular, but has come under much criticism for not being safe. If you find aluminum wiring, tell your client to contact an electrician immediately.

Well, you've done it. You've just inspected your first house. Hope you enjoyed it. Like one inspector we talked to told us: it sure beats a day job! Of course, in your case you didn't get paid for this first inspection. But you will get paid for the next, and the next, and the next...

In Conclusion

The local library can be invaluable to your new business. They have books on every subject including framing houses, heating systems, landscaping, etc., that will help you learn your new trade. They also have books on running a business, work processing, and tax computation that will be extremely helpful for the business end. Take these books out, read them, copy drawings from them, look for new techniques or services that you can offer that may make your business just a little better than your competitor's business. Who knows, in a few years when you are an expert home inspector, you may want to write the newest book on home inspection!

We have included a number of books and periodicals in our Resources section. Most of these we found at the local library, some at book stores.

Good luck with your new business.

Home Inspection Checklists

Address _____

City/State/Zip _____

Client _____

Phone _____

	TYPE/STYLE/MATERIAL	CONDITION			COMMENTS

EXTERNAL

		Excellent	Good	Poor	
Foundation_____		☐	☐	☐	_____
Grading_____		☐	☐	☐	_____
Drainage_____		☐	☐	☐	_____
Driveways_____		☐	☐	☐	_____
Walkways_____		☐	☐	☐	_____
Patios_____		☐	☐	☐	_____
Pool/Jacuzzi_____		☐	☐	☐	_____
Landscaping_____		☐	☐	☐	_____
Steps/Porch_____		☐	☐	☐	_____
Fences/Walls_____		☐	☐	☐	_____
Roof_____		☐	☐	☐	_____
Chimney_____		☐	☐	☐	_____
Gutters/Downspouts_____		☐	☐	☐	_____
Flashing_____		☐	☐	☐	_____
Outside Lighting_____		☐	☐	☐	_____
Garage_____		☐	☐	☐	_____
Other_____		☐	☐	☐	_____

INTERNAL

ATTIC

Insulation _____		☐	☐	☐	_____
Vents_____		☐	☐	☐	_____
Insects_____		☐	☐	☐	_____
Chimney_____		☐	☐	☐	_____
Dampness_____		☐	☐	☐	_____
Other_____		☐	☐	☐	_____

BEDROOMS

Floor_____		☐	☐	☐	_____
Walls_____		☐	☐	☐	_____
Windows_____		☐	☐	☐	_____
Ceiling_____		☐	☐	☐	_____
Electrical Outlets_____		☐	☐	☐	_____
Closets_____		☐	☐	☐	_____
Doors_____		☐	☐	☐	_____
Other_____		☐	☐	☐	_____

TYPE/STYLE/MATERIAL	CONDITION			COMMENTS
LIVING ROOM/FAMILY ROOM	Excellent	Good	Poor	
Floor _____	☐	☐	☐ _____
Walls _____	☐	☐	☐ _____
Windows _____	☐	☐	☐ _____
Ceiling _____	☐	☐	☐ _____
Electrical Outlets _____	☐	☐	☐ _____
Closets _____	☐	☐	☐ _____
Doors _____	☐	☐	☐ _____
Other _____	☐	☐	☐ _____
DINING ROOM				
Walls _____	☐	☐	☐ _____
Windows _____	☐	☐	☐ _____
Ceiling _____	☐	☐	☐ _____
Electrical Outlets _____	☐	☐	☐ _____
Closets _____	☐	☐	☐ _____
Doors _____	☐	☐	☐ _____
Other _____	☐	☐	☐ _____
KITCHEN				
Walls _____	☐	☐	☐ _____
Windows _____	☐	☐	☐ _____
Ceiling _____	☐	☐	☐ _____
Electrical Outlets _____	☐	☐	☐ _____
Closets _____	☐	☐	☐ _____
Doors _____	☐	☐	☐ _____
Counter Tops _____	☐	☐	☐ _____
Plumbing _____	☐	☐	☐ _____
Other _____	☐	☐	☐ _____
KITCHEN APPLIANCES				
Stove _____	☐	☐	☐ _____
Oven _____	☐	☐	☐ _____
Clock _____	☐	☐	☐ _____
Timer _____	☐	☐	☐ _____
Microwave _____	☐	☐	☐ _____
Vent/Hood/Fan _____	☐	☐	☐ _____
Garbage Disposal _____	☐	☐	☐ _____
Dishwasher _____	☐	☐	☐ _____
Refrigerator _____	☐	☐	☐ _____
Freezer _____	☐	☐	☐ _____
Trash Compactor _____	☐	☐	☐ _____
Wet Bar _____	☐	☐	☐ _____
Other _____	☐	☐	☐ _____

TYPE/STYLE/MATERIAL	CONDITION			COMMENTS

BATHROOMS

	Excellent	Good	Poor	
Floor _____	☐	☐	☐	_____
Walls _____	☐	☐	☐	_____
Windows _____	☐	☐	☐	_____
Ceiling _____	☐	☐	☐	_____
Electrical Outlets _____	☐	☐	☐	_____
Closets _____	☐	☐	☐	_____
Counters _____	☐	☐	☐	_____
Sinks _____	☐	☐	☐	_____
Tub _____	☐	☐	☐	_____
Shower _____	☐	☐	☐	_____
Toilet _____	☐	☐	☐	_____
Plumbing _____	☐	☐	☐	_____
Fan/Skylight _____	☐	☐	☐	_____
Other _____	☐	☐	☐	_____

GARAGE INTERNAL

Floor _____	☐	☐	☐	_____
Walls _____	☐	☐	☐	_____
Windows _____	☐	☐	☐	_____
Ceiling _____	☐	☐	☐	_____
Electrical Outlets _____	☐	☐	☐	_____
Garage Door Opener _____	☐	☐	☐	_____
Insulation _____	☐	☐	☐	_____
Other _____	☐	☐	☐	_____

HOT WATER HEATER

Type/Capacity_____	☐	☐	☐	_____
Main Shutoff Valve _____	☐	☐	☐	_____
Water Supply _____	☐	☐	☐	_____
Water Pressure _____	☐	☐	☐	_____
Mounting _____	☐	☐	☐	_____
Venting _____	☐	☐	☐	_____
Plumbing Fixtures _____	☐	☐	☐	_____
Pipes _____	☐	☐	☐	_____
Leakage/Rusting _____	☐	☐	☐	_____
Other _____	☐	☐	☐	_____

TYPE/STYLE/MATERIAL	CONDITION			COMMENTS

HEATING SYSTEM — Excellent / Good / Poor

	Excellent	Good	Poor	
Type Of Heat _____	☐	☐	☐ _____
Type Of Fuel _____	☐	☐	☐ _____
Heating Plant _____	☐	☐	☐ _____
Thermostat _____	☐	☐	☐ _____
Filters _____	☐	☐	☐ _____
Venting _____	☐	☐	☐ _____
Burner Type/Condition _____	☐	☐	☐ _____
Ducts _____	☐	☐	☐ _____
Leakage/Rusting _____	☐	☐	☐ _____
Other _____	☐	☐	☐ _____

BASEMENT/SLAB

	Excellent	Good	Poor	
Walls _____	☐	☐	☐ _____
Floor _____	☐	☐	☐ _____
Insulation _____	☐	☐	☐ _____
Dampness _____	☐	☐	☐ _____
Wiring _____	☐	☐	☐ _____
Venting _____	☐	☐	☐ _____
Heating Ducts _____	☐	☐	☐ _____
Other _____	☐	☐	☐ _____

FIREPLACES/CHIMNEYS

	Excellent	Good	Poor	
Firebricks _____	☐	☐	☐ _____
Gas Jets _____	☐	☐	☐ _____
Flue _____	☐	☐	☐ _____
Damper _____	☐	☐	☐ _____
Chimney _____	☐	☐	☐ _____
Roof Spark Arrester _____	☐	☐	☐ _____
Weather Shield _____	☐	☐	☐ _____
Pipes _____	☐	☐	☐ _____
Leakage/Rusting _____	☐	☐	☐ _____
Other _____	☐	☐	☐ _____

ELECTRICAL

	Excellent	Good	Poor	
Fuses/Circuit Breakers _____	☐	☐	☐ _____
Amps _____	☐	☐	☐ _____
Circuits _____	☐	☐	☐ _____

ADDITIONAL REMARKS

_____

_____

_____

_____

Housing Construction Terminology

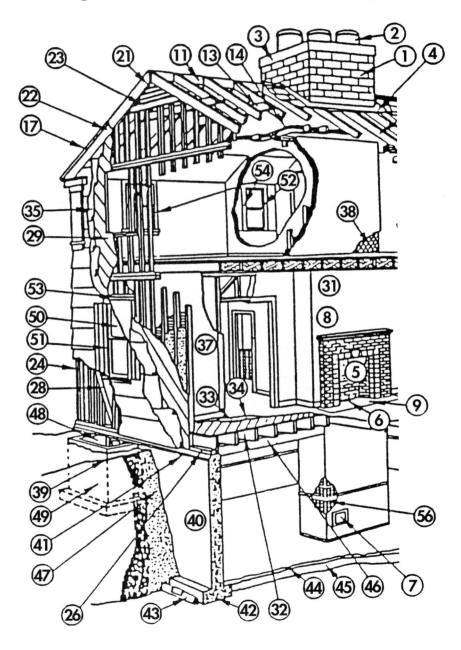

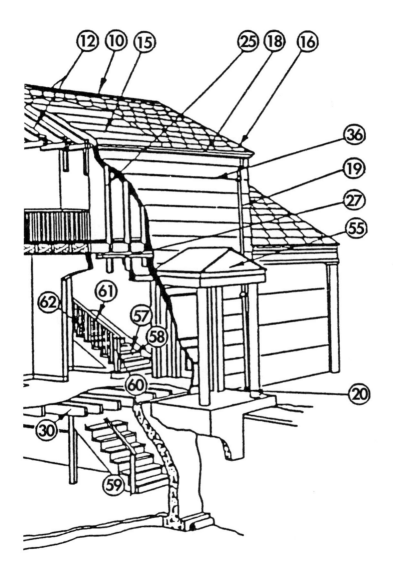

Housing Construction Terminology

A. Fireplace

1. **Chimney:** A vertical masonry shaft of reinforced concrete or other approved noncombustible, heat-resisting material enclosing one or more flues. It removes the products of combustion from solid, liquid, or gaseous fuel.

2. **Flue Liner:** The flue is the hole in the chimney. The liner, usually of terra cotta, protects the brick from harmful smoke gases.

3. **Chimney Cap:** This tap is generally of concrete. It protects brick from the weather.

4. **Chimney Flashing:** Sheet-metal flashing provides a tight joint between chimney and roof.

5. **Firebrick:** An ordinary brick cannot withstand the heat of direct fire, and so special firebrick is used to line the fireplace.

6. **Ash Dump:** A trap door to let the ashes drop to a pit below, from where they may be easily removed.

7. **Cleanout Door:** The door to Erie ash pit or the bottom of a chimney through which the chimney can be cleaned.

8. **Chimney Breast:** The inside face or front of a fireplace chimney

9. **Hearth:** The floor of a fireplace that extends into the room for safety purposes.

B. Roof

10. **Ridge:** The top intersection of two opposite adjoining roof surfaces.

11. **Ridge Board:** The board that follows along under the ridge.

12. **Roof Rafters:** The structural members that support the roof.

13. **Collar Beam:** Not really a beam at all. A tie that keeps the root from spreading. Connects similar rafters on apposite side of roof.

14. **Roof Insulation:** An insulating material (usually rock wool or fiberglass) in a blanket form placed between the roof rafters for the purpose of keeping a house warm in the winter, cool in the summer.

15. **Roof Sheathing:** The boards that provide the base for the finished roof.

16. **Roofing:** The wood, asphalt, or asbestos shingles - or tile, slate or metal - that form the outer protection against the weather.

17. **Cornice:** A decorative element made up of molded members usually placed at or near the top of an exterior or interior wall.

18. **Gutter:** The trough that gathers rainwater from a roof.

19. **Downspouts:** The pipe that leads the water down from the gutter.

20. **Storm Sewer Tile**: The underground pipe that receives the water from the downspouts and carries it to the sewer.

21. **Gable**: The triangular end of a building with a sloping roof.

22. **Garage Board**: The fascia or board at the gable just under the edge of the roof.

23. **Louvers**: A series of slanted slots arranged to keep out rain, yet allow ventilation.

C. Walls and Floors

24. **Corner Post**: The vertical member at the corner of the frame, made up to receive inner and outer covering materials.

25. **Studs**: The vertical wood members of the house, usually 2 x 4's generally spaced every 16 inches.

26. **Sill**: The board that is laid first on the foundation, and on which the frame rests.

27. **Plate**: The board laid across the top ends of the studs to hold them even and rigid.

28. **Corner Bracing**: Diagonal strips to keep the frame square and plumb.

29. **Sheathing**: The first layer of outer wall covering to the studs.

30. **Joist**: The structural members or beams that hold up the floor or ceiling, usually 2 x 10's or 2 x 12s spaced 15 inches apart.

31. **Bridging**: Cross bridging or solid. Members at the or third points of joist spans to brace one to the next and to prevent their twisting.

32. **Subflooring**: The rough boards that are laid over the joist. Usually laid diagonally.

33. **Flooring Paper**: A felt paper laid on the rough floor to stop air infiltration and, to some extent, noise.

34. **Finish Flooring**: usually hardwood, of tongued and grooved strips.

35. **Building Paper**: Paper placed outside the sheathing, not as a vapor barrier, but to prevent water and air from leaking in. Building paper is also used as a tarred felt under shingles or siding to keep out moisture or wind.

36. **Beveled Siding**: Sometimes called clapboards, with a thick butt and a thin upper edge lapped to shed water.

37. **Wall Insulation**: A blanket of wool or reflective foil placed inside the walls.

38. **Metal Lath**: A mesh made from sheet metal onto which plaster is applied.

D. Foundation and Basement

39. **Finished Grade Line**: The top of the ground at the foundation.

40. **Foundation Wall**: The wall of poured concrete (shown) or concrete blocks that rests on the footing and supports the remainder of the house.

41. **Termite Shield:** A metal baffle to prevent termites from entering the frame.

42. **Footing:** The concrete pad that carries the entire weight of the house upon the earth.

43. **Footing Drain Tile:** A pipe with cracks at the joints to allow underground water to drain in and away before it gets into the basement.

44. **Basement Floor Slab:** The 4- or 5-inch layer of concrete that forms the basement floor.

45. **Gravel Fill:** Placed under the slab to allow drainage and to guard against a damp floor.

46. **Girder:** A main beam upon which floor joists rest. usually of steel, but also of wood.

47. **Backfill:** Earth, once dug out, that has been replaced and tamped down around the foundation.

49. **Areaway:** An open space to allow light and air to a window, also called a light well.

49. **Area Wall:** The wall, of metal or concrete, that forms the open area

E. Windows and Doors

50. **Window:** An opening in a building for admitting light and air. It usually has a pane or panes of glass and is set in a frame or sash that is generally moveable for opening and shutting.

51. **Window Frame:** The lining of the window opening.

52. **Window Sash:** The inner frame, usually moveable, that holds the glass.

53. **Lintel:** The structural beam over a window or door opening. Also called a header.

54. **Window casing:** The decorative strips surrounding a window opening on the inside.

F. Stairs and Entry

55. **Entrance Canopy:** A roof extending over the entrance door.

56. **Furring:** Falsework or framework necessary to bring the outer surface to where we want it.

57. **Stair Tread:** The horizontal strip where we put our foot when we climb up or down the stairs.

58. **Stair Riser:** The vertical board connecting one tread to the next.

59. **Stair Stringer:** The sloping board that supports the ends of the steps.

60. **Newel:** The post that terminates the railing.

61. **Stair Rail:** The bar used for a handhold when we use the stairs.

62. **Balusters:** Vertical rods or spindles supporting a rail.

17

Personnel: Hiring Employees

Wile home inspection is the perfect one-person business, you may find yourself in the near future with more work than you can handle. This will be especially true if you are located in a part of the country that has a booming real estate market. Contractors will be too busy to want to bother with inspections, and lenders will be really anxious to get the home in and out of escrow and into the hands of the buyer.

When this happens you may want to consider an assistant. There are several things to bear in mind, though, when considering hiring someone.

First, you will want someone who is willing to work just as hard as you do. They should be in fairly good physical shape, because they will be climbing stairs, ladders and poking in and out of crawl spaces. They must like working with people and be willing to get along with even the most irate clients. And they must be well organized.

You'll want to choose someone that will properly represent you and your business philosophies. It is probably better if this is not a friend. While many successful business relationships have resulted in some beautiful lifelong friendships, many others have failed because the friends' relationship got in the way of the business relationship.

You may want to consider hiring a contractor or handyman. As we mentioned earlier this can be a plus for some clients, especially if they already have their heart set on the house that you are inspecting. If your firm can offer not only a complete, honest (and we can't stress this enough)

> *Knowledge is of two kinds. We know a subject ourselves or we know where we can find information on it.*
>
> *Samuel Johnson*

home inspection, but also offer speedy repairs after the purchase, then your business will take on another facet that can mean increased work and increased profits.

Selecting Candidates

Have interested applicants fill out a standard employment application (as shown on the following pages) and provide references from former employers and business associates. Do not just take the information provided at face value; check these references very carefully to find out about the applicant's sense of loyalty, responsibility and honesty. This can be done by phone or with a letter.

In either case, request answers to specific questions dealing with those factors that are most important to your job requirements; in this case promptness, character and

Employment Application

The Janson Co.
34659 Virginia Road
Anytown, USA 94635

Please Print

As an equal opportunity employer, our company policy as well as federal, state, and city laws, prohibits discrimination in employment based on race, color, religion, sex, national origin, age, or physical handicaps unrelated to job performance.

General

NAME Last First Middle	SOCIAL SECURITY NUMBER

PRESENT ADDRESS Street City State Zip	TELEPHONE NUMBER	EMERGENCY NO.

PREVIOUS ADDRESS Street City State Zip	LENGTH OF TIME AT ADDRESS

POSITION DESIRED	SCHEDULE PREFERRED	
	FULL-TIME ☐ PART-TIME ☐	Are you related to anyone employed by this company?
REFERRED BY		YES ☐ NO ☐
		Name _____
DATE AVAILABLE		Relationship _____
SALARY DESIRED $		Position _____

Employment History (Most Recent Employer First)

EMPLOYMENT	NAME AND ADDRESS OF EMPLOYER	POSITION/RESPONSIBILITIES
FROM		
TO	SUPERVISOR TELEPHONE NO.	
SALARY	REASON FOR LEAVING	
FROM		
TO	SUPERVISOR TELEPHONE NO.	
SALARY	REASON FOR LEAVING	
FROM		
TO	SUPERVISOR TELEPHONE NO.	
SALARY	REASON FOR LEAVING	

Employment Application

Education

	NAME AND ADDRESS	NO. OF YEARS	YEAR GRAD.	SUBJECTS STUDIED
HIGH SCHOOL				
TRADE OR BUSINESS SCHOOL				
COLLEGE OR UNIVERSITY				
OTHER				

FOREIGN LANGUAGES SPOKEN

References (List the names of three persons not related to you.)

NAME & ADDRESS	JOB TITLE	YRS. KNOWN	TELEPHONE

Skills (Check the applicable areas in which you have experience.)

☐ TYPING   ☐ WORD PROCESSING   ☐ SPREADSHEET   ☐ EPBX, PBX
WORDS PER MINUTE _____ ☐ DATA PROCESSING   ☐ 10-KEY ADDING MACH.   ☐ DICTAPHONE

LIST APPLICABLE   WORD PROCESSING _____   SPREADSHEET _____
SOFTWARE PACKAGES: DATA PROCESSING _____   GRAPHIC _____

CHECK COMPUTER SYSTEMS WITH   ☐ IBM   ☐ MACINTOSH
WHICH YOU'RE EXPERIENCED: ☐ IBM-COMPATIBLES   ☐ OTHER _____

LIST OTHER SKILLS YOU POSSESS:

Additional Information

HAVE YOU EVER SERVED IN THE UNITED STATES ARMED FORCES? ☐ NO ☐ YES
If yes, give years of service and final rank:

HAVE YOU EVER BEEN CONVICTED OF A FELONY OR A MISDEMEANOR? ☐ NO ☐ YES
If yes, explain in detail:

I certify that all information provided on this application is correct to the best of my knowledge. I understand that willful omission or deliberate falsification of this information is grounds for termination.

APPLICANT'S SIGNATURE: _____ DATE: _____

Sample Follow-Up Letter

The Janson Co.
34659 Virginia Road
Anytown USA 94635

Joan Anderson
Staffing & Employment Department
34659 Virginia Road
Anytown, USA 94635

Dear Applicant:

Thank you for applying for a position with the Janson Co. We welcome your interest in our organization.

We continually evaluate candidates' backgrounds and interests against our current personnel requirements. Be assured we'll review your experience and you'll be notified within 10 working days if your qualifications appear to meet our current needs. If there is not a current match, your application will be kept in our files and reviewed as future openings occur.

Again, thank you for your interest in the Janson Co.

Sincerely,

Joan Anderson
Staffing Administrator

courtesy, dependability, work habits and loyalty. Be wary of candidates who list friends or relatives as references; they could be trying to conceal unfavorable information.

The Interview Process

Schedule a personal interview to make your own determination based on poise, appearance, level of interest in the job, abilities and future goals. Write out any questions you may have ahead of time to help you stay on track.

Set up the interview in a comfortable place to put the candidate at ease. For example, if you operate out of your home, arrange to meet at a convenient location during a slow time, or if you have an office, set it up when you won't be bombarded by phone calls or people stopping in. In addition to finding out about their capabilities and goals, you will want to use this time to talk about the company, your expectations, standards and, of course, the pay structure. In this case you might also want to devise a simple test related to the candidate's knowledge of the job.

On-the-Job Training

When you find someone who seems to have all the qualifications needed, arrange to train them on the job. Many owners like to do this themselves, to ensure that their standards are instilled from the beginning and to get a first-hand idea of the new recruit's work habits.

If you have a trusted employee on staff, have the new recruit accompany them on assignments to learn the ropes. This extra duty should always result in a bonus for the employee doing the training.

Training may take several weeks or months, depending on the worker's previous experience. Basically, a good training process should involve the following steps:

- Gain the recruit's confidence by putting him or her at ease.
- Find out what he or she already knows.
- Indicate the importance of each aspect of brokering a deal.
- Explain and show each step patiently.
- Be sure each step is understood before moving on to another.
- Encourage and welcome questions.
- Have the recruit try to do the task.
- Correct mistakes gently.
- Have him or her repeat the steps to you.
- When you are both comfortable, let the recruit go out alone.
- Review performance periodically.
- Offer support by letting the employee train others when ready.

Taking time to train properly reduces turnover, improves the quality of work performed and in addition lowers your cost of labor.

Overtraining the Ambitious

Sometimes, it is possible to train someone so well they feel they can start their own business in competition with yours. This occasionally happens when employees realize you are making money off their hard work. There are several ways to stay on top of your employees' activity.

If you're certain an employee is thinking of starting their own business, take him or her aside and explain the administrative aspects of the business. Find out if they truly realize what you are doing for them in terms of finding work on a continual basis and if they understand how much is involved in running their own business.

In rare cases, you are going to lose employees who feel confident enough to start their own business and there isn't too much you can do about it.

In other situations, you can "promote" the employee by making him or her a "senior executive" or sales manager, as appropriate. This is feasible only if your cash flow and the employee's ability warrant it.

The Benefits of Happy Employees

Personnel management is a time-consuming job for business owners. However, paying attention to the needs of your employees and working to gain their trust and maintain loyalty can do nothing but benefit your business.

The attitude of your employees about your management techniques plays an important part in building and maintaining your reputation in the community.

If employees are treated fairly and with respect, their job satisfaction will be reflected in the way they do their job.

This is something that can truly keep you ahead of the competition; a loyal, efficient and enthusiastic group of workers is one of your most effective forms of public relations, so never scrimp when it comes to keeping your employees happy. A few important rules of thumb in dealing with employees include the following:

• Never expect an employee to do something that you wouldn't do.   This is why training new recruits your self is such a good idea; it shows them that you are willing and able to step in and do anything required if necessary.

• Listen to your employees and incorporate their ideas whenever it is feasible. Suggestions that work for the

good of the company should be rewarded with
a bonus.

• Take the time to talk about business standards and
practices so that everyone knows exactly what is
expected of them. Outline duties and responsibilities
on the job and schedule regular reviews to ensure that
they are constantly met. If you find it necessary to
talk to an employee about their work habits, do it in
private so they are not embarrassed in front of their
peers. And do not criticize; merely offer constructive
ways that they can improve their performance.

• Treat each employee as an individual. When someone seems to be having personal problems that are
interfering with their ability to work, be willing to
allow them time off without penalty to take care of the
situation. An employee plagued with problems may
carry them into the client's home or to the event site
and this would have a negative effect. It is much
better to get someone to fill in until the regular
employee is operating at full efficiency again.

• If a particular client is having a personality conflict
with an employee, assure the employee that it isn't
their fault and point out the benefits to everyone
involved of sending in a replacement.

18

ADVERTISING YOUR BUSINESS

More than 150 years ago, Thomas Macaulay, a British historian and statesman, said, "Advertising is to business what steam is to industry. [They provide] the same propelling power."

Few in business would argue with Macaulay's observation—it is as true today as it was when steam was the driving force behind industry. But the question remains, "How do you get the most out of your advertising dollar?" The answer is to: a) know your customer, b) target your market and c) understand the basics of advertising.

This section discusses the various aspects of advertising, including how to use circulation figures to figure your cost per thousand (CPM) and how to create ads that will bring results.

What Is Advertising?

Advertising informs the public about:

- Who you are,
- What kind of business you operate,
- How they can buy your products or services, and
- Why they should come to you.

Before you even open the doors of your business, you should start thinking about your advertising program—how much money you can afford to spend, where your dollars will be best spent and how to structure your campaign.

Decide what kind of results you expect. Are you looking for immediate sales or ongoing recognition? What kind of customers are you hoping to attract? Are you emphasizing price, service, workmanship or something unique? Once you have answered these questions, your decision as to the best type of advertising for the allotted dollars will be easier to make.

There are three basic types of advertising that you will be most interested in during the first few years of your business.

Start-Up Advertising: This includes your business cards and stationery, the flyers and brochures you have created to announce your new business, and your initial newspaper advertising campaign. Your main focus here will be on telling people where you are located and what you can offer them.

Ongoing Advertising: Once the business is "up and running," so to speak, it will be vital to your success to institute a regular advertising campaign that is well-planned and, this is the key, consistent. Your goal, at this point, is to attract new clients, obtain repeat business from existing clients, and enhance your reputation.

Looking Good: After you have reached the point where your business is on steady ground and showing increased profits every year, you can afford to dabble in "institutional advertising," as it is called in the trade. This is where you pick up the tab to send a dozen kids to the rodeo when it comes to town or sponsor a float in the local Fourth of July parade and, in return, get your name listed on the program or on a banner in the parade. This is primarily name recognition only and, while every little bit is helpful, by the time you can afford it, you probably will be in pretty good shape anyway.

Yellow Pages

Few successful operators claim that they can build their businesses strictly by word-of-mouth referrals. If you're planning to structure a full-scale operation, placing a listing in the Yellow Pages is an absolute necessity.

This requires installing a business telephone, which is equally important if starting the business from home. Calling for service and having a child, for example, answer the phone will kill any interest a potential client may have.

Check with the Yellow Page Directory Advertising Representative of the telephone company to find out when the directory in your area is published. Since they come out at different times during the year depending on the region, it may be necessary to develop a supplemental newspaper advertising or other promotional campaign.

If, for example, you are planning to open for business in August and the phone book in your area comes out in March, you do not want to lose eight months of valuable exposure to prospective clients by doing nothing during that period of time.

Direct Mail

Another way to target specific markets is through direct mail using brochures, flyers, and other materials outlining your home inspection business and detailing the benefits of using your operation. These days direct mail is a more expensive proposition because of postage, but if you mail only to select groups or zip codes within your city to pull the best response, it can be worthwhile.

Mailing lists, broken down by zip codes, income brackets and other specific factors, can be purchased inexpensively from some printers, even small print shops in your city, advertising agencies, local publications and mailing list brokers, all of which are listed in the Yellow Pages.

If you do institute a direct mail program, be sure to send regular announcements to those who've responded to ads in the past but didn't buy your goods or use your service.

Circumstances frequently change, and sending reminders that you are still in business offering quality service at a fair price is sure to result in response at some point.

Just be aware that the average return for direct mail is between 2% and 5% and don't expect the phone to ring off the hook every time you send a mailing. Consistency is the important factor here.

Specialty Items

Specialty advertising serves as an effective reminder. Specialty advertising refers to the matches, pens, key chains and similar items that have a company's name printed on them . . . every time you use the item, you think about the firm, even if it is subconscious.

Investigate the kind of items you can have printed by visiting a specialty advertising representative (listed in the telephone book under "Advertising"). Notepads, pens, pencils, and desk calendars are among your best forms of specialty advertising.

Classified Ads

Don't underestimate the power of classified ads. Many major corporations utilize the classifieds even though they have sizable budgets available for display advertising.

There are several reasons for this:

1) The classifieds are an extremely reliable testing ground for new products, services, and ideas. Although it's true that people who typically "read" the classifieds are a different group from those who scan display ads, they are considered to be responsive and, therefore, can give you a very good idea of whether or not you have placed your ad in the appropriate publication.

2) A short, well-written classified placed in the right publication and under the proper category can be a low-cost method of advertising that guarantees solid returns.

3) If a company is trying to establish a mailing list, a classified ad that features an "Inquiry" statement such as "Send name & address for free details (or a brochure)" is a good way to build up a file of qualified buyers' names. And they can be considered qualified buyers because it takes time, energy and the cost of a postage stamp for them to get your free information. By writing to you they have stated their interest.

4) Classified ads are inexpensive, ranging from 50 cents to $15 per word, depending on the publication. With careful planning, you should be able to get broad-based coverage without putting a dent in your operating capital.

Display Advertising

As with all types of advertising, it is important to define your market when getting ready to place a display ad. Your main goal should be to select a publication that will reach the audience you want and then create a specific ad that appeals to that target group.

To Write or Not to Write?

Writing display ad copy is not for the inexperienced. Although it is possible to learn how to put ideas and words together that will get the results you desire, it is recommended that you hire a copywriter if you have any qualms about producing an ad.

However, if you are confident that you can develop your own ad, remember that it must generate interest through the use of carefully planned words and design.

When planning your ad, keep the following elements in mind:

a) *Visibility.* Your ad may well be surrounded by many others, so make sure it immediately attracts the reader's attention.

b) *Boldness.* Use large art and/or a bold headline as a focal point.

c) *Simplicity.* Don't overwhelm the reader with too many fine details. The ad's main point is lost and so is the reader's attention. This is particularly true in a small ad.

d) *White space.* Just because you have, say, a 4 x 6 inch space to work with, it isn't necessary to fill it up with graphics. White space is a necessary component in assuring your ad will be read.

e) *Use legible typestyles.* The easiest to read are Times Roman and Bookman (the type used in this business guide), which are known as serif typefaces because of the tiny strokes at the tops and bottoms of the letters. Sans serif (without strokes) type such as Helvetica are okay for ads containing few words, but are difficult for the eye to follow when there is a lot of text. Also, be sure that the type is large enough—generally nothing smaller than 10 point type should be used.

Design and Typesetting

It isn't necessary to be a great artist to create an ad, especially these days with the availability of impressive graphic materials, including cut-out and transfer (press-on) letters in different type faces, symbols, borders and design ideas through graphic art supply companies, such as Formatt and Chartpak. Also, most word processors contain computer graphics that can really dress up your ad at a low cost.

If you feel uncomfortable about laying out your ad so it has eye appeal, consider hiring an art student to handle the job for a prearranged fee or as a school assignment (talk with the head of the art department to see if they have a work/study for credit program). Just be sure to review the student's work prior to making a commitment.

Also, check with the advertising department of the newspaper or magazine you are planning to advertise in. There may be graphic artists

> *Advertising is the greatest art form of the 20th Century.*
>
> *Marshall McLuhan*

or designers on staff who will work on the layout for you. In fact, there still are newspapers in the country that offer full services, from ad concept to design work, at minimal charge to clients.

Publications work on tight deadlines so be sure you start the process early enough to get a proof copy of your ad back in time to make any corrections. You can imagine the frustration of seeing your ad appear with the wrong address. Although the publication would probably do a "make-good" for you and run a corrected ad at no charge, the damage has already been done. The final responsibility for the ad rests on you, so plan ahead.

Tracking Ad Response

Some customers will tell you that they saw your ad and might even let you know what they liked or disliked about it. They will probably be in the minority, however, so you must develop methods for determining if your advertising is working for you.

One very simple way is to include a coupon for something in the ad and to count the number of coupons you get within a certain test period after the ad runs. There is one major problem with this, however. Even the most well-intentioned people often cut coupons, file them away in a "safe" place and totally forget about them.

So, although you will be able to gauge response to some degree, be aware that many of the people who come into or call your business have probably seen the coupon, but simply mislaid it or are not the kind of folks who use them.

Predicting Response

There is a standardized formula in advertising which provides a barometer for predicting how much response can be expected from either a display or classified ad. The formula states that you will see 1/2 of the total responses from an ad within a certain period of time after receiving your first inquiry or order. For an ad to run in a daily newspaper, the period of time is 3 days; for a weekly newspaper or magazine, it is 6 days; the period is roughly 15 days for a monthly publication, and within 25 days when running in a bi-monthly. Although there are exceptions, this provides a base from which to track response.

Determining Your Cost per Thousand (CPM)

The CPM equation helps you develop a cost-effective campaign. Basically, it tells you what your ad cost per 1,000 readers will be.

Most publications will provide a CPM comparison upon request (some include it in their media kits), but you can easily figure it out for yourself with just a few facts from publications you are exploring as advertising vehicles.

For convenience sake, CPM equations are typically based on the rate of a full-page black and white ad. You simply divide the full-page rate by the thousands of the overall circulation. It's important that you get the circulation, not the readership, as magazines and newspapers typically claim that their readership is 2 to 50 percent higher because of "pass-along" of the publication to friends.

For example, if a certain newspaper is charging $2,000 for a full-page ad and they claim their true circulation is 200,000, you will be paying $10 per 1,000 readers for your ad space. Another specialized publication's full-page rate may be $1,000 with a circulation of 50,000. The cost per 1,000 readers will be much higher— $20 per 1,000, but it might be worth it if, for example, you have a unique product or service that is geared to an exclusive market.

Benefits of Paid Circulation

It is also important to know that publications with a paid circulation generally have a readership that is more inclined to respond to advertising. This is because of the simple fact that they are a captive audience who have taken the time to order the publication. This is especially valuable if you ever have a product or service that you're planning to market through mail order.

You can find circulation, readership demographics, advertising rates and other important information about a number of publications (especially those with national distribution) through Standard Rate and Data (SR&D) or the Ayer Directory of Publications (and their monthly updates), available through the research desk at your local library.

Recently, the Advertising Research Foundation and the Association of Business Publishers conducted a study to determine the impact of advertising on the sale of products.

Several different products were used for the study and each was advertised for a 12-month period in an appropriate publication. The results were interesting, but not surprising to anyone who has ever utilized a solid advertising campaign in promoting their business.

- More advertising meant more sales.
- Determining results from an ad campaign generally took 4 to 6 months. (One or two insertions does not indicate viable results.)
- Color in advertisements dramatically increased response and sales.
- A well-developed ad campaign kept on working for a year and sometimes even longer in publications with a high "keep" appeal.

Knowledge and belief in your service, faith in yourself and respect for your customers are the keys to successfully building your future. As you go about starting up and establishing your business, remember the word "profit." This alone should give you the necessary motivation to get out there and confidently tell the world what you have to offer.

Promotion and Public Relations

Informing the public about your business through the use of business cards, brochures, mailing pieces, and specialty items such as desk calendars, pens, and note pads imprinted with your company name, is a form of advertising that is known as promotion.

The things you can do over and above your paid advertising and promotion that help build your image and keep your business in the public consciousness are referred to as public relations. It is a fine line in terminology, but can make or break your business if not addressed.

There are many clever ways to extend the effectiveness of your advertising and promotional dollars, as illustrated in the following examples.

A Little Creativity Goes a Long Way

The owner of a pet grooming business leaves a business card and a brochure featuring a 20% discount coupon everywhere he goes. When he is running errands, he always takes a handful of brochures with him to hand to store clerks, gas station attendants and waitpersons he runs into along the way.

If he sees a car with a dog in it, or one with a bumper sticker announcing the owner's affection for their pet, he slips a brochure under the windshield wiper. Does it work? Absolutely. He claims that 45% of his new business is from the recipients of his handouts and the majority of them become regular customers.

Another business owner who operates a small walking tour service in her beachside town sends out a one-page quarterly newsletter featuring historical and other facts about the area to everyone who has ever taken the tour. She includes a $10 coupon, which can be redeemed by former clients or their guests.

She states that many of her clients are local residents who send their out-of-town visitors on her walking tour, simply because she makes sure they are aware that she is still in business and generates enthusiasm through the newsletter.

Charity Tie-Ins

Other ideas you might consider include promoting human-itarian outreach. For example, for every ten referrals to your service, you donate a predetermined amount of money to a local charity. You can easily keep track of their purchases by punching a hole at the edge of a card designed by you or your printer strictly for that purpose.

When you are ready to present the check to the par-ticular charity, make sure the chairperson of the organiza-tion is going to be available to accept it and be sure to con-tact the local press and invite them to the "event." In most cases, they will give you free coverage.

Reminder Cards

Sending regular "thinking-of-you" cards to your past and present clientele is especially effective with service busi-nesses. Again, it assures the customer that you are friend-ly, reliable and successful—a real plus for your credibility.

> *Advertisements contain the only truths to be relied on in a newspaper.*
>
> *Thomas Jefferson*

Networking

Check out local business-owners groups and the chamber of commerce in your area. Pay your membership dues and join as many as possible. Membership offers you the opportunity to meet people who might use your service, and will, at bare minimum, tell others about you once they know you, feel comfortable and understand what you are offering. You will also be given a listing in the group's directory, generally under your specific category. And, as is so often the case, the members are prone to supporting others involved with their group. It is quite possible that members with compatible businesses will put a stack of your cards or brochures on their counter or in their referral file. In return, you may be able to promote their businesses to your customers. This is the true meaning of "networking."

The directory also gives you bonafide access to an instant mailing list, which you can use to send out promotional flyers or brochures. Participating in their events and the willingness, for example, to speak at functions about your area of specialization will let people know that you are community-minded. This involvement will work to project a positive image for you and your business.

Customer Service

One of the most overlooked areas in promoting business is the impression we create when dealing with customers. The ageless philosophy that the customer comes first and is always right has, it seems, gotten lost in the shuffle in these days of fast-paced, fast-buck dealings from Main Street to Wall Street.

As a small business owner, it is guaranteed that customers will flock to you if you make them feel important. It is as easy as greeting them warmly (instruct your employees, if you have them, to do the same), maintaining a courteous attitude and inviting them to come back soon—even if they have not used your services.

Word travels fast and if you create an atmosphere that makes each and every person you deal with feel like the only person in the world, you can be sure they will tell their friends and neighbors.

Free Publicity

Free publicity also comes under the category of public relations. This includes articles and interviews in newspapers and magazines or coverage on radio and television, featuring interesting or unusual facts about you and your business.

As any newspaper reporter or talk show host will tell you, everybody has a story to tell. The key is to get the media to zero in on yours and make it available to the public. If you have trouble deciding on a unique angle for your story, invite several friends over for a brainstorming session to create a newsworthy item.

> *The advertisement is one of the most interesting and difficult of modern literary forms.*
>
> *Aldous Huxley*

Use your imagination to explore the creative possibilities of your business venture. And then look at your personal story. Perhaps you have completely switched fields with your new business. That represents a story angled toward risk-taking. Maybe you have successfully turned a hobby into a business venture, or created a unique product or developed a new twist on an old theme.

These all qualify as human interest stories. Newspaper and magazine editors love them—almost as much as their readers enjoy them.

Once you have your story angle, call the managing editor or the feature editor of the newspaper. Give him or her a brief description of who you are and what business you are in. Tell them you will be sending out a press release and would be happy to arrange an interview at their convenience.

Invite them to visit your place of business and get a firsthand look at what you are doing and how you're doing it. Do the same with program directors or talk show hosts at regional television and radio stations, offering your availability.

If, on the first attempt, your presentation fails to result in an article, follow up in three to six months, possibly with a new story angle. In the meantime, however, send out regular press releases announcing new developments with your business—the grand opening, special events, details on your business philosophy, extra services and features. Even if they don't run a full story on you alone, there is a good likelihood they will include you in a feature story about local entrepreneurs or people in similar businesses.

An Effective Ad Campaign

All of the methods outlined above, along with others you will develop, keep your name in the consumer's mind. The effectiveness of an advertising/publicity campaign can be measured by conducting a simple marketing survey with new customers. Make it standard practice to ask them where they heard about you and your business.

Keep a tally of the responses in a notebook. A periodic review will give you hints of where to allocate future advertising funds. If, for example, the majority of your customers are being drawn from your direct mailings to potential clients, keep them going on a steady basis. The same principle applies to Yellow Pages display ads, specialty ads or word-of-mouth advertising.

The justification for investing in advertising and promotion is time. If you attempted to contact all of the people who read ads and press release material in newspapers or those who listen to talk shows, you would never have time to conduct your business . . . you would be too busy recruiting.

It can't be stressed enough: Time is money. As a small business owner, you will want to devote as much attention as possible to the production end of your venture and let your advertising and promotion work to bring in the customers.

19

RESOURCES

Industry Sources

Being Self-Employed, An All-Year Tax Guide, Holmes F. Crouch

The Complete House Inspection Book, Don Fredriksson

Getting a Good House—Tips and Trick for Evaluating New Construction, Bob Syvanen

The Home Inspection Handbook, Howard Hugh for Home Renovation Associates

House Inspection—A Buyer's Guide, Dale Chaney and Jeff Miller

How to Buy a House in California, Ralph Warner, Ira Serkes, George Devine

How to Buy a House/How to Sell a House, Joel Makower

J.K. Lasser's Your Income Tax

National Electrical Code, National Fire Protection Association (NFPA), Quincy, MA

Plumbing for Dummies, Don Fredriksson

Residential Inspection Techniques, Don Fredriksson

The Stanley Complete Step-by-Step Book of Home Repair and Improvement, James A. Hufnagel, Editor

Uniform Building Code, ICBO, Whittier, CA

Uniform Mechanical Code, International Association of Plumbing and Mechanical Officials, IAPMO, Los Angeles, CA

Uniform Plumbing Code, IAPMO, Los Angeles, CA

Uniform Solar Energy Code, IAPMO, Los Angeles, CA

Uniform Swimming Pool, Spa and Hot Tub Code, IAPMO, Los Angeles, CA

Wiring Simplified, H.P. Richer, W.C. Schwan

General Reference Books & Periodicals

"A Consumer's Guide to Telephone Service," Consumer Information Center, Pueblo, CO 81009

AT&T 800-number information. Call 1-800-272-0400.

Bacon's Publicity Checker: A comprehensive listing of every major newspaper in the United States and Canada. Available through the Research Desk at your local library.

Encyclopedia of Associations. Published annually by Gale, Detroit. Available through the Research Desk at your local library.

Encyclopedia of Business Information Sources: Published periodically by Gale, Detroit.

Home Magazine, 44th Floor, 1633 Broadway, New York, NY 10019

National Five-Digit ZIP and Post Office Directory, Address Information Center, 6060 Primacy Parkway, Memphis, TN 38188-9980.

Remodeling, Washington, DC, (202) 452-0800

Remodeling News, Ramsey, NJ, (201) 327-1600

Roget's Thesaurus in Dictionary Form (Synonyms and antonyms)

Superintendent of Documents, Government Printing Office, Washington, DC, 20402 (Request listing of publications)

Tax Guide for Small Businesses. Internal Revenue Service Publication #334. Published annually. Available from local IRS office.

Ulrich's International Periodicals Directory. Comprehensive listing of major magazines and newspapers. Available through the Research Desk at your local library.

Walls and Ceilings, Tampa, FL, (813) 989-9300

Webster's New Collegiate Dictionary, Published by G & C Merriam Company, Springfield, MA.

Where to Find Business Information by David Brownstone and Gorton Carruth. (Publisher: John Wiley & Sons, New York)

Your Home, Ogden, UT, (801) 394-9446

Small Business Associations & Government Agencies

American Marketing Association, 250 South Wacker Drive, Chicago, IL, 60606-5819 (Marketing publications available to non-members.)

Bureau of the Census, Washington, DC, 20233. (Statistical data)

Copyright Office, Library of Congress, 101 Independence Avenue SE, Washington, DC 20559 (Information on copyrighting written and visual materials.)

Council of Better Business Bureaus, 4200 Wilson Blvd.Suite 800, Arlington, VA. 22203 (Ask for a listing of their "Booklets on Wise Buying.")

Dun & Bradstreet, 299 Park Avenue, New York, NY, 10171. (Send for the booklet "This is Dun & Bradstreet," an overview of publications and services.)

International Franchise Association, 1350 New York Avenue NW, Suite 900, Washington, DC, 20005. (Regulation and information on franchises.)

Minority Business Development Agency, Office of Public Affairs, Department of Commerce, Washington, DC 20230

National Association for the Self-Employed, P.O. Box 612067, DFW Airport, Fort Worth, TX, 75261-2067.

National Association of Women Business Owners, 600 South Federal Street, Chicago, IL, 60605.

National Federation of Independent Business, 150 West 20th Avenue, San Mateo, CA, 94403.

National Insurance Consumers Organization, P.O. Box 3243, Merryfield, VA 22116-3243. (Send self-addressed stamped envelope for free booklet, "Buyer's Guide to Insurance.")

National Minority Business Council, Inc., 235 East 42 St., New York, NY 10017 (Quarterly newsletter for small & minority business.)

National Small Business United, 1155 15th Street NW Suite 910, Washington, DC, 20005. (Send for info on federal legislation for small businesses.)

National Trade and Professional Associations of the United States. Available through the Research Desk at your local library.

Occupational Safety & Health Administration (OSHA), Department of Labor, Washington, DC 20210. (Employment regulations.)

Office of Information and Public Affairs, U.S. Department of Labor, 200 Constitution Ave NW, Washington, DC, 20210 (Request publications list regarding employment.)

Small Business Administration, 1441 L Street NW, Washington, DC, 20416. (For booklets and information on the Service Corps of Retired Executives — SCORE.)

INDEX

A

Accountants, 97-98
  fees, 98
Additional operating expenses, 123
Ad response, tracking, 208
Advertising, 201-16
  classified, 205
  cost per thousand (CPM), 201
  defined, 202-3
  design/typesetting, 207-8
  direct mail, 204
  display, 206-8
  effective ad campaign, 215-16
  institutional, 203
  ongoing, 202
  response, predicting, 208-9
  specialty, 204-5
  start-up, 202
  writing, 206-7
  Yellow Pages, 203
  See also Promotions/public relations
Area wall, 188
Areaway, 188
Ash dump, 184
AT&T, 46
Attorneys, 96-97
  fees, 97
  as markets, 29
Auctions, 90-91
Automatic redial, telephone systems, 45
Ayer Directory of Publications, 210

B

Backfill, 188
Balance sheet, 123, 141, 147-48
Balusters, 189
Banks, approaching for financing, 130
Bank statement reconciliation, 141, 148-49
Basement floor slab, 188
Beveled siding, 187
Binoculars, 81
Bookkeeping:
  debit/credit in, 143
  double-entry, 141-42
  single-entry, 142
Brainstorming, 110-11
Break-even point, 152-53
Bridging, 187
Briefcase, 70

Brochure, 30, 204
Building paper, 187
Business cards, 30, 70, 113-14
Business deductions, 102-3
  local taxes, 103
  state income tax, 103
Business meetings, minimizing, 166-67
Business name, 109-16
  brainstorming, 110-11
  business cards/stationery, 113-14
  fictitious name statement, 111
  visual image, 111-13
Business phone line, 66
Business plan, 117-24
  advantages of, 118-20
  financial statements, 122-24
  key questions to ask yourself, 120-22

C

Calculator, 87
Call forwarding, 45
Call waiting, telephone systems, 45
Candidates, selecting, 192-96
Carbon monoxide detector, 82
Cash Flow Statement, 70, 72-73, 126
Cash journal, 141
  example of, 145-46
CD-ROMs, 86
Census Bureau, and regional statistics, 35
Charity tie-ins, 212
Chimney, 184
Chimney breast, 184
Chimney flashing, 184
Classified ads, 27, 205
Cleanout door, 184
Collar beam, 185
Commercial lenders, 128-30
  approaching, 130-31
Commercial location guidelines, 48-51
  area demographics, 48
  competition, 48-49
  image, 49
  inspection location, 52-54
  lease, 51
  manufacturing businesses, 50
  products/service, 49
  rent required, 49-50
  retail businesses, 50
  service businesses, 50
  traffic patterns, 49